Smoothing Irons

A HISTORY AND COLLECTOR'S GUIDE

Brian Jewell

Published By

Wallace-Homestead Book Co.
1912 Grand
Des Moines, Iowa 50305

By the same author
Veteran Sewing Machines
Model Car Collecting

In the same Midas Collectors' Library
Veteran Talking Machines
Scales and Balances (in preparation)
Stoneware Jars and Pots (in preparation)
Coin Operated Machines (in preparation)
Tin Plate and Enamelled signs (in preparation)
Motor Badges and Figureheads (in preparation)

First published 1977 by
MIDAS BOOKS
12 Dene Way, Speldhurst,
Tunbridge Wells, Kent TN3 0NX

© Brian Jewell 1977

ISBN 0 85936 076 8 (Casebound)
ISBN 0 87069 221 6 (Paperbound)

Printed in Great Britain
by Errey's Printers Ltd, Heathfield, Sussex.

Contents

An illuminated address from the employees. Dated June 19, 1891, the headlines read 'The Centennial Celebration of the establishment of the firm of Archibald Kenrick and Sons.' The testimonial records the firm as having 1200 employees. Photograph: Archibald Kenrick & Sons Limited.

INTRODUCTION

There exists a love-hate feeling for the smoothing iron. Without doubt they are attractive artefacts and well suited to collecting. Some even possess beauty and are fine examples of craftsmen's skills, on a similar level to clocks and articles forged from precious metals. But pleasing craftsmanship cannot change what they are—tools of drudgery, to use according to fashion's whim. How many women's tears, one wonders, have tested the heat of the iron's sole. The housewife or maidservant did not look upon a newly acquired iron with pleasure and pride as she would on say, one of the products of Mr. Isaac Merritt Singer or Messrs Willcox and Gibbs. On the contrary, the smoothing iron, a symbol of female subservience, brought the dread anticipation of ordeal to come, like the sight of the cane to a delinquent child standing in the master's study.

The fact that irons have been produced in so many styles makes them an ideal subject for collecting. Even the largest are reasonably compact and take up less space than many other collectibles. One lady collector keeps her irons on the steps of her staircase.

Smoothing irons have been seriously collected long enough for there to have been a number of books written on the subject, but the surprising and sad fact is that very little has been published. Dealers and others are remarkably ignorant—in 1975 a dealer, in business for at least fifteen years, told the author she had no idea about the purpose of a simple polishing iron she had in her shop. And polishers were common up to 1939! We have seen standing irons described as wig stands, and even charcoal irons of makes in current production catalogued as antiques at auctions.

It is hoped this book will clear up a few misconceptions and promote more research into smoothing irons and domestic iron founding in general. The only apology to be made is for the gaps in information. One day, perhaps, the definitive work will be written; until then it is necessary to hunt for any details, marks on irons of all types, old ironmongery catalogues and industrial directories.

We owe a considerable debt of gratitude to the late A. H. Glissman of Carlsbad, California, a foremost collector and authority on irons who, in 1970, wrote and published *The Evolution of the Sad Iron*. This was a strictly limited edition of 1,000 copies and an important collector's piece in its own right apart from being an invaluable reference.

The author is anxious to receive any information about marques and manufacturers not included, as well as further details and points of controversy about those listed in the Directory section.

Tunbridge Wells, 1977

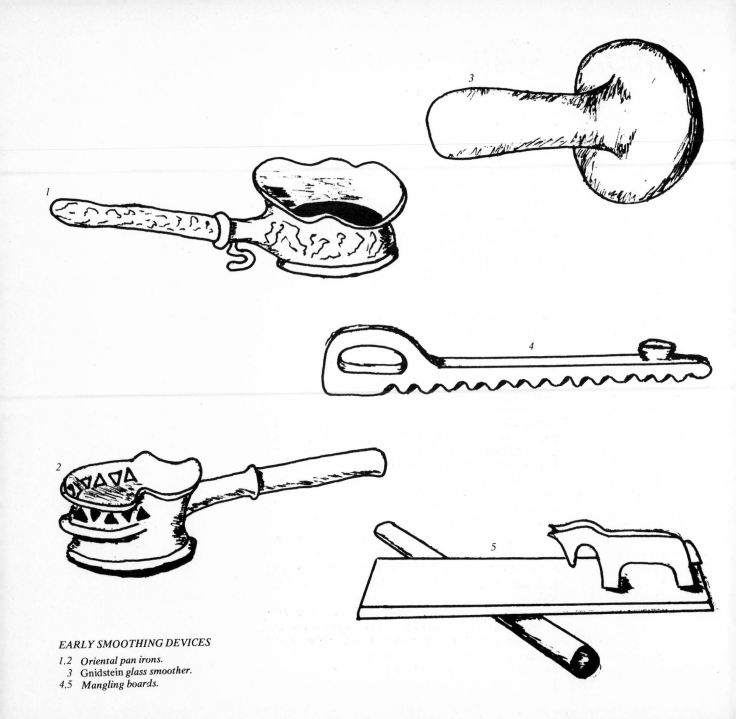

EARLY SMOOTHING DEVICES

1,2 Oriental pan irons.
  3 Gnidstein *glass smoother.*
4,5 *Mangling boards.*

Chapter One

HISTORY: PANS, BOARDS, BOXES AND SADS

Cosmetic smoothing of household linen and clothing could begin only when flax, cotton and silk came to be spun into thread fine enough for the finished woven articles to react favourably to the application of a heated tool.

It is believed that, like many other inventions, the Chinese were responsible for the introduction of the smoothing iron. There is some pictorial evidence for this belief. The late A. H. Glissman in *The Evolution of the Sad Iron* draws attention to a painting in the Museum of Fine Arts, Boston, reputed to be the work of the Emperor Hui-Tsung (1082-1135), showing a woman smoothing some cloth with an open-pan iron of similar type to those still used in oriental countries. The artist is said to have used as a model a picture from the eighth century. If we are to accept these dates as authentic, then this must be the first recorded use of an ironing device. (Fig. 1, 2, 46)

On the other hand we cannot dismiss the *slikjikjakje* and *gnidestein* finds in the early graves of Scandinavian women. These objects, 'cow's jaw bone' and 'rubbing stone' respectively, were used cold on damp linen, as were the black glass smoothers which were made until the latter part of the eighteenth century. (Fig 3).

The glass smoothers were adequate for most items of clothing but very hard work when it came to large flat household articles. The Northern European solution came in the shape of the mangling board and roller. First the cloth was rolled as smooth as possible with the roller in the same way as pastry is flattened with a rolling-pin then, while still damp, the cloth was wound on the roller and pushed back and forth on the table with the mangling board. In this way quite a remarkably high laundering standard could be achieved. (Fig 4. 5).

The introduction of the mangling board probably came in the sixteenth century and was used by Scandinavian, German and Dutch housewives until well into the nineteenth century. They were also taken to far flung places by emigrants and colonists, in particular to the Dutch settlements in America, South Africa and Indonesia.

While most mangling boards had a smooth under-surface, some were corrugated. Often they were very decorative and excellent examples of folk art. It was customary for a swain to present his bride-to-be with a mangling board which he had lovingly fashioned and carved; a custom which has its parallel in the giving of carved wooden *love spoons* in Wales.

6   *Box iron of Isaac Wilkinson design.*

These early European methods of smoothing, unlike the Chinese pan-irons, did not use heat. The oriental iron is therefore the more genuine ancestor of smoothing irons.

It was in the early part or around the middle of the sixteenth century that the idea of using a hot iron to smooth cloth occurred to Europeans, the Dutch seemingly pioneering the method. Starting from about this period, the irons themselves fell into two basic classifications: the *box iron* into which a pre-heated iron slug had to be placed, and the *sad* or *solid iron* that had to be heated on a stove. Which came first is a matter of speculation, but it is reasonable to suppose that it was the box iron—the earliest surviving examples are of this type. If the idea of using heat came from the East, there was a model to work on, and on which to base a skilled trade—that of the iron maker. The Dutch formulated a four-year apprenticeship before the iron maker could be called a master. At the same time blacksmiths, unskilled in the specific craft of making smoothing irons, were probably inundated with orders from those who could not afford the high price of a hand-fashioned brass bodied box iron. The blacksmith would take a piece of iron, hammer it into an imitation of the boat-shaped work of art from the master-craftsmen's workshops, a handle was attached and there it was, the poor man's—or rather woman's—new prestige symbol, only it had to be heated on the stove. But to repeat, this period of smoothing iron history is a matter for conjecture, the fact is two types of smoothing irons have come down to us.

The early Dutch irons were elegant brass boxes adorned with profuse relief and engraved decoration. The handles were of equally artistic form with floral or scroll motif. Manufacture spread to other European areas, notably Scandinavia, Germany and France, each nation's iron makers developing their own characteristic styles.

The heating agent was an iron slug, heated in a fire and placed in the iron with tongs through a lift-up or swing gate at the rear. The slugs were in pairs, one in the iron and the other heating in the stove.

Box smoothers of wrought iron were also made from the early seventeenth century, particularly in Germany and Britain. English irons, both sad and box, were usually of cast steel or iron rather than brass. Although the first British patent for a box iron was granted to Isaac Wilkinson of Bersham, Denbighshire in 1738—very early as patents go—it is certain that irons were made for a long time before that date. (Fig 6). Apart from Wilkinson, the early British makers of series-production irons—as opposed to the one-off craftsman-article—included Izons (foundry active 1760-1940) and Kenrick who started making irons in 1791.

The earliest discovered record of an iron heated by a fire burning within it, is in Morland's painting *The Beautiful Ironing Girl* of the 1780s.

Fire-burning box irons need both means for air to get in and for smoke to escape—the latter passing through more holes along the sides of the box or through the chimney set in the top plate. Often these holes were highly ornamental, in stepped and floral shapes, the complexity depending on the skill of the iron maker. Top plates or lids were hinged or removable and held in position with a latch. And still are for that matter, for they continue to be made in and for a number of countries where electricity is a source of power for the privileged few. (Fig 7, 8)

As Mr Glissman stated in *The Evolution of the Sad Iron,* it is difficult to trace early records of American made irons. He notes that the first known iron casting for domestic use was a kettle made in Lynn, Mass., in 1644, but the earliest documentary evidence on smoothing irons does not appear until 1784, when there are records of a delivery to Hope Village, Pennsylvania.

Making up for lost time, and with typical American ingenuity, smoothing iron related inventions came thick and fast in the nineteenth century, particularly from the 1850s onwards, and it was from the New World that fresh thinking stemmed—the first innovations since the appearance of the European box and sad irons in the sixteenth century.

From the middle of the nineteenth century in the U.S.A. the slug-heated box iron, although still made, declined in popularity in favour of the charcoal burning iron. The industry concerned with the production of smoothing irons spread through the States at a speed paralleled only by that of sewing machine manufacture from the mid-1850s and, years later, the production of the automobile. In the year 1856, one foundry alone, that of Bless & Drake in Newark, N.J., produced some 100,000 irons and, although the largest at that time, they were but one of very many manufacturers.

At first sight it may seem that little could be done to improve box, sad and charcoal irons, and it is a testimonial to the genius of nineteenth century American inventors that they found so many flaws in the basic conception to justify the granting of the enormous number of U.S. patents covering improvements and changes in design:- Better means of controlling draught and thereby the heat generated by the charcoal—there was even a patent granted in 1856 covering an iron which incorporated bellows to increase the burning rate of the charcoal. (Fig 31). Irons that were designed to burn nuggets of coke. Irons that looked more like today's pressure-cookers than laundering tools (Fig 122). Irons cast in the shapes of swans and railway locomotives. (Fig 38). Better insulation to the handle. These were all reasons for a patent application.

Of all the American patented improvements in design, one stands out above all others. This is the design of Mary Florence Potts of Ottumwa, Iowa. She saw the big disadvantage of the sad iron as being the fact that it had to be heated on a stove and, while this was being done, the handle became too hot to hold. Mrs Potts conceived the notion of making the handle detachable so that only the body of the iron need be subjected to heat. (Fig 164). The patent covering this invention was granted on the 4th of April 1871, just over a year after she had received her first patent for a sad iron with points at both ends. Together, the two inventions made such an

7

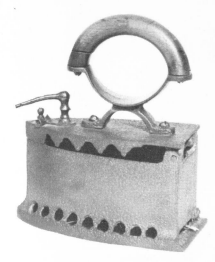

8

7 *Edna charcoal iron.*
8 *Charcoal iron with Austrian style handle.*

advance in sad iron design that it is surprising that the old shield-shape (it's funny that in Heraldry this is called the *heater* shape), with fixed handle survived at all after the expiration of the Potts' patent.

Mary Potts assigned her licence for manufacture first to the Chalfant Manufacturing Company in Pennsylvania, and, subsequently, to the Enterprise Manufacturing Company, and the American Machine Company. The *Mrs Potts Patent Cold-Handle Sad Iron* was made in the other leading industrial nations of Britain, Canada, Denmark and Germany, as well as by a large number of foundries in the U.S.A. after the patent had run its course. Archibald Kenrick & Sons of West Bromwich, held the English licence in 1880 (Fig 45), the year of the granting of the final renewal of the U.S. Patent.

In Germany, the great iron foundry of Grossag at Schwabisch-Hall, made the Potts iron up to a few years ago, while in the U.S.A. the last manufacturer to produce the design was the Colebrookdale foundry in Pennsylvania, who ceased making it in 1953—101 years after they had commenced the making of smoothing irons.

9

10

9   *British-made Mrs. Potts cold-handle iron.*
10   *A Mrs. Potts iron in brass.*

Chapter Two

HISTORY: TURNING ON THE HEAT

This part of the history of smoothing irons is fraught with danger. Not only was it hazardous to use the fuels burned in some of the self-heating irons, but even writing about them is to invite confusion. The names given to fuels in one country can mean something completely different in another. In the U.S.A., *coal gas* is called *natural gas,* and *petrol* is still called *gasoline* and often simply *gas.* What the English call *paraffin* was first termed *coal oil* in the U.S.A., and later *kerosene.* It is hoped that this book will go some way to 'iron out' a few misunderstandings and not provoke them.

Box irons with coal gas (natural gas in U.S.A.) burners seem to have been used in the United States either in or before the 1850s, as the patent application of David Lithgow, Philadelphia (1858) (Fig 11) refers to previous methods of heating irons in this way—he may, of course, have meant that one could simply place a sad iron over a gas flame to heat it! Gas for lighting was first used in the U.S.A. in 1820, and in England it was as early as 1792, so it is reasonable to suppose that gas was an early alternative to solid-fuels for irons. There are in existence some really antique-looking gas irons from English and Danish factories (Fig 12), but as the basic design of the gas iron changed very little until well into the twentieth century, it is difficult to put a year to any specific example.

Lithgow's patent gas iron and the European made models were of the self-heating variety but there were other irons designed to utilise coal gas. These were heated over a gas jet with the flame applied to the top plate to avoid sooting the sole. These irons usually had a hole in the handle so it could be placed in an inverted position on the bracket.

Before mineral oil was taken out of the ground in volume in the 1860s, first for lighting and heating, and then to provide fuel for the internal-combustion engine, the world depended on vegetable oil: *colza* or *rape-seed* oil as it was called. Even in the 1870s, France still had 400,000 acres down to kale from which the seed-oil was derived. One can imagine the economic upset when mineral oil started to flow (or should it be slurp) in the power arteries of transport and industry. Some French sad irons had a lip around the edge for retaining seed-oil which, when burning, would heat the body of the iron. These French irons are reminiscent of the ancient open seed-oil and grease lamps which probably the Romans brought to Gaul and Britain.

From colza to paraffin (kerosene) was a logical progression. Paraffin,

11

12

11 *David Lithgow, U.S.A. 1858.*

12 *Rostell & Rekard, Denmark. Early nineteenth century.*

13

14

15

13   German-made 'Brilliant' spirit iron.
14   'Fuluse' self-heating travelling iron with stand and 'meta' fuel.
15   'Fuluse' iron in heating positon.

derived from shale or coal tar, has similar burning characteristics to vegetable oils. It is therefore surprising that it took some while for the first paraffin heated iron to appear, sometime in the 1890s.

Naphtha would seem a strange and deadly fuel for heating an iron but the design for such a device was patented in the U.S.A. in 1868. It is not known if it went into production.

Safer burning agents were methylated spirits and alcohol, and here we have a rich field for the collector. In the main they were compact companion-irons for travellers, often with the secondary purpose of heating water—those were the days before running h & c in hotel bedrooms. However, there was at least one spirit iron designed primarily for household laundry. This was the subject of a U.S. patent granted in 1854, the invention of one Jeremiah Brown of Hartford in Connecticut. It was an ingenious design with the spirit lamp inside the iron, heating the upper surface while the lower surface was being used. When cool the entire body was turned over so the top plate became the sole. (Fig 84).

Of all the spirit irons the most ubiquitous was that of Josef Feldmeyer of Wurzurg, Germany. This was called *The Brilliant*. (Fig 13). It had the classic lines of a much earlier German box—come to think of it, it's quite possible that Feldmeyer modified an old iron for his purpose when making the prototype and the production examples retained the same style. The sides were pierced to allow the intake of air and a fuel tank was carried at the rear with the fuel pipe going through a hole in the gate, the flow being controlled by a valve. If Feldmeyer did modify a sad iron for his experiments he would have been following the example of Karl Benz when he fitted his internal-combustion engine to a carriage designed to be pulled by horses.

The Brilliant was patented and manufactured in a number of countries, including Britain and the U.S.A., where Feldmeyer was granted patents in 1897 and 1900. It was also made in Belgium, France and Italy. In Germany, his design was exploited by several companies including the Omega works at Thuringia—a great foundry whose production of smoothing irons could be matched in Germany only by Grossag.

Use of solidified methylated spirit cubes (meta) was the next step in development of the travelling iron and it was much more convenient to carry the cubes than a bottle of spirit. The design of these portable irons usually included a separate base casting wherein the fuel was burned and upon which the iron proper rested in an inverted position to be heated. The complete assembly could be used for heating water or even warming food.

Carbide-acetylene gas heated irons were fairly late in arriving on the market, or so it seems, for this author has found no evidence of the existence of such irons before the first three or four years of the present century.

Petroleum (*gasoline* in the U.S.A.) heated irons were in series production in the early years of the twentieth century by manufacturers in both Europe and the United States. Petrol has either to be vaporised by heat, mixed with air and then ignited, or it is fed under pressure to a chamber where it is mixed with air. Either way it is a tedious business but Tilly in Britain and Coleman in the U.S.A. both of whom made petrol-burning lamps, persisted with their products up to this generation.

Electricity came to ironing in the 1880s. In the U.S.A., the patent granted on Oct 30, 1883 to Dyer and Seely was probably the first. (Fig 16). This was a cordless iron which had to be placed on a special stand with sprung connectors in order to be charged with electricity to heat the element. In Europe, about the same time, inventors favoured a flexible cable attached to the iron by open terminals. (Fig 17). Whichever system the housewife chose, one thing was certain—there would be a few shocks to come.

16

17

16   *Dyer & Seely iron. c.1884.*

17   *English made electric iron. 1880s.*

The factory of Archibald Kenrick & Sons
Limited, West Bromwich, c.1885. The border
shows the company's departments. Photograph:
Archibald Kenrick & Sons Limited.

Chapter Three

HISTORY: THE DICTATES OF FASHION

Of course, it would be true to say that all smoothing irons owe their existence to fashion and style. After all, the human would be little worse-off in baggy and wrinkled clothes if everyone looked the same. But man, proud man (and woman, no less), dressed in a little brief authority or not, has demanded smooth, crisp attire. Hence the smoothing iron.

Styles of costume through the ages have called for, and received, different patterns of irons. The obliging inventors have always been there to fill the need. Some inventions can lead the world into craze or habit (the motor car for example), others are destined to sit on the train of popular demand. The special purpose irons are such inventions, as are all tools other than the most sophisticated and gimmicky, and those seldom last.

An early example of a special purpose iron, which is really but a branch of the family tree, is the *goffering iron* intended to form the intricate ruffles and tucks that abound on sixteenth century costume. The iron to attend to the starched ruffs was developed in Italy and, for some time, it was known as the *tally iron* (a shortening of the word *Italy*). Later, when the French used it for fluting and crimping, *tally* was dropped in favour of *goffering*—a corruption of the French word for such trivia, *gaufrer*. The goffering iron comprised an upright stand, projecting from which was one or, more often, several various sized cylinders, each closed at one end. (Fig 18). A heated poker-like iron was inserted into the open end of the barrel and, when sufficiently warm, the duly starched material to be treated ⸱ould be smoothed over the barrel with the fingers, one tuck at a time. Indeed a long and tedious process.

Towards the close of the nineteenth century, several manufacturers were producing scissor-like irons for putting flutes into the material. Some of these irons looked like fire-heated hair curling tongs, while others were multi-pronged and capable of putting in more than one flute at a time. (Fig 19). Fluting irons and fluting machines to make multiple pleats were the direct descendants of goffering irons. They were introduced just after the middle of the nineteenth century and inventors had decidedly varying ideas on the form the tool should take. Some were machines that stacked the pleat-folded and dampened cloth in place until it dried in its creases. (Fig 20). Others were of a flat-bed type with wooden slats that pressed the cloth into recesses. (Fig 33). There were corrugated rollers that meshed into ridges on a

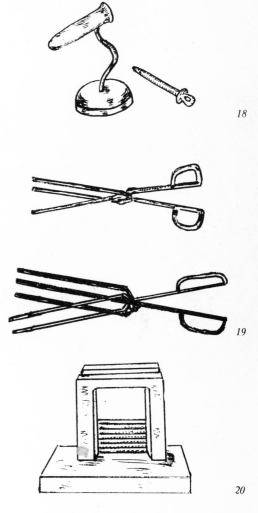

18

19

20

18 Goffering or 'tally' iron.

19 Examples of fluting or quilling tongs.

20 A 'stacking' type fluting machine.

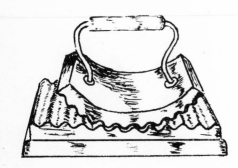

21

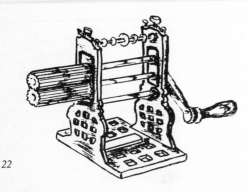

22

21   *'Geneva' hand fluter. 1866.*

22   *Thomas Clark's Warranted Crimping
Machine. Made in England.*

board, (Fig 21) and still others that gave the appearance of miniature wringers. (Fig 22). But the true fluting iron was a regular smoothing iron with a fluting attachment, a tool that few Victorian households were without. (Fig 43).

There seems to have been almost as many makes and styles of fluters as there were plain smoothing irons and, whichever way achieved, the result was the same—pleats to satisfy the fashion of the day.

Puffed sleeves and bustles needed ironing from the inside and their shapes would present considerable problems to anyone using an ordinary smoothing iron, especially one of the large box or charcoal burning types. For these parts of garments special egg-, ball-, or mushroom-shaped irons were evolved in the early nineteenth century. (Fig 23-6). These were either fixed on upright stands or were hand-held. The business end was heated and the material drawn over the ball. Standing irons are still in production incorporating steam jets for use in laundries, and smaller versions are available for the home.

It was the vogue in the nineteenth century for starched garments such as shirts to be finished with a high sheen. This was achieved by applying heavy pressure with a rounded surface, and special irons were made accordingly. (Fig 47). The polishing iron had either convex sole or rounded edge, the principle being that the smaller the contact area and the greater the pressure applied, the higher would be the sheen on the garment. One American inventor went so far as to patent a two-handled iron so more of the operator's body weight could be brought to bear. (Fig 32).

Most polishing irons had smooth soles but there were exceptions. The American inventor, Michael Mahony, was granted a patent in 1876 covering an iron with an overall relief-patterned sole, the rounded edges of the pattern giving the required sheen.

Like the fluters, polishers were made by many manufacturers in a wide variety of styles.

The English foundry of J. & J. Siddons continued to produce a polishing iron until the outbreak of the second World War, but by then trubenized collars and a new fashionable soft look were taking the starch out of life to some extent and, after the war, nobody thought it worthwhile to make polishing irons. That is a provocative statement and, even as it is being typed this author imagines the 'feedback' letters after publication informing him of the foundries still making polishers. Perhaps it would be best to add the time-honoured play safe phrase, 'according to presently held information'.

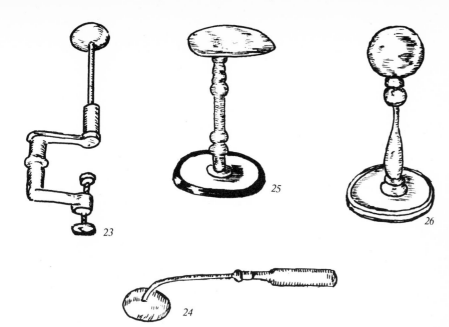

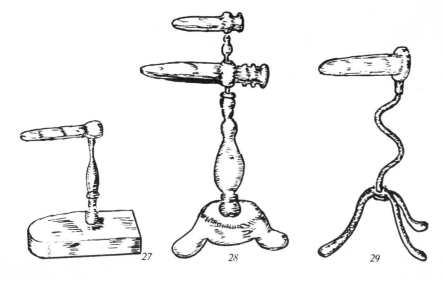

23   *Clamp-on-table egg iron. The iron is
       detachable from the base for use with
       a handle.*

24   *Egg iron with handle.*

25   *Mushroom standing iron.*

26   *Ball standing iron.*

27-29 *Goffering or Italian ('tally') irons.*

Chapter 3
History:
The Dictates
of Fashion.

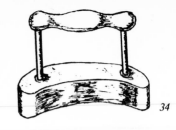

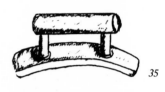

30 'The Only Base Burner' 1898.

31 Taggart's charcoal iron with bellows. 1856.

32 The Prentis polishing iron. The interior
    core is lifted out for heating.

33 A flat-bed fluting machine.

34 Hatter's 'tolliker'.

35 Hatter's 'matrisse'.

36 Mary Cook's Polishing Iron. c.1849.

37 Colt carbide acetylene gas iron, U.S.A.

From left to right: *A c.1900 spirit iron from the Omega foundry in Germany, in the style of* The Brilliant *designed by Josef Feldmeyer. An English made electric iron of the 1880s. A hard-to-date box iron of the style of Isaac Wilkinson, made in England from 1738 until 1940. A box iron, probably of German origin—the handle and gate suggest it was made in the late eighteenth century.* Photograph: Broadwater Collection.

HOW TO MAKE A FORTUNE.

You want to know how I made my fortune! Well! it's very simple! You know as well as I do that accidents and a little smartness have been the parents of many fortunes and inventions. Well, one day my wife was ironing out on the borders of a forest in the far West, our log hut being too small for the work. She had to leave the job for a few minutes and ask me to mind the things. Now in this forest were a great number of monkeys, and, compelled by natural imitativeness, one of the monkeys went to the ironing-board, took up an iron, and commenced ironing. Then an immense idea struck me. I calculate there is money in this, said I. If I were to put a number of ironing boards and irons out here I guess the monkeys would do our ironing for nothing. No sooner thought than done. So I went to all the large towns in the vicinity and made contracts for all the laundry work, and having no wages to pay I could do it very cheap. Then I returned, and spread out a lot of ironing boards all over the forest, as well as the self-heating "Dalli" Box Iron, and it was all right, I tell you. A great crowd of monkeys at once swooped down upon the irons, and started ironing like mad from morning till night. I made my great pile through this, and bought the land, built a city, which in gratitude to this instrument which helped to achieve all this, I called 'The 'Dalli' Town.' This gigantic success could never have been accomplished without the "Dalli" Box Iron, which can be used without gas or fire in the open or anywhere.

The "DALLI" is acknowledged the most up-to-date and best Box Iron, doing away with the worries of the old system. No Gas, no Fire, no Smell. Hot in a few minutes and remains hot. No changes of Irons. Self-heating with Smokeless Fuel. Can be used anywhere without interruption, even out of doors, doing double the work in half the time. More economical than any other iron. Price of the "Dalli" is **6/-**. Price of the "Dalli" Fuel is **1/9** per box of 128 Blocks. To be had of all Ironmongers or Domestic Stores. If any difficulty apply to—

THE DALLI SMOKELESS FUEL CO., 27, Milton Street, London, E.C.

*38   A sad iron in the shape of a locomotive
was patented in 1888 by American
inventor, E. B. Cosby. It is not known if
the iron went into production.*

Chapter Four

TERMS AND TYPES

Over the centuries iron makers have created a language of their own. Many of the terms and descriptions are neither self-explanatory nor precise and can be confusing.

The following short dictionary will, it is hoped, go some way towards clarification.

ALCOHOL IRONS. See Spirit Irons.

BILLIARD TABLE IRONS. These are large rectangular-soled sad irons. They are provided with a metal shoe to keep the cloth clean. These irons are usually cast for, and marked with, the name of the billiard table makers, for instance: BURROUGHES & WATTS, LONDON. (Fig 39).

BOX IRONS (also known as Slug Irons and Heater Irons). Known from the sixteenth century and still made in the twentieth century, box irons were the first known type of smoothing device. As the name suggests, they are metal boxes, pointed at the front and squared at the rear where there is a lifting or swing gate through which the pre-heated slug of iron is inserted.

Box irons were first made by the Dutch who had a four year apprenticeship for their iron makers.

The early box irons were cast brass but cast iron was not unknown. Later, box irons—from late eighteenth century—are almost invariably of cast iron. (Fig 40, 41)

CARBIDE-ACETYLENE IRONS. Marketed in the early years of the twentieth century, carbide-acetylene heated irons did not enjoy the same wide popularity as bicycle lamps using the same fuel. The reason is probably the characteristic smell given off by the gas. (Fig 37)

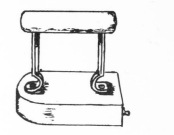

CARPET IRONS. Archibald Kenrick & Sons Limited of West Bromwich were among the manufacturers of very heavy sad irons, some weighing as much as 32 pounds, for use on carpets.

CHARCOAL IRONS (also known as Ember Irons). A development of the slug-heated box iron. To heat the slug iron, hot embers were taken from the fire and placed in the body casting. The lids are hinged either at the rear or, after c.1850, sometimes at the side.

The weight is usually between 6 and 7 pounds. (Fig 42)

ELECTRIC IRONS. First made in the 1880s. In the U.S.A. the first

39   *Billiard table iron made for Burroughes & Watts of London.*

40   *German box or* bolt. *Early nineteenth century.*

41   *Danish round-nosed box iron in brass. The style is early seventeenth century.*

42

43

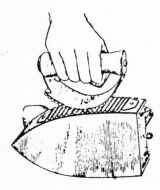

42   *Kaltschmidt. c.1925.*

43   Mode d'emploi *for the fluting attachment on the Pease combined fluting and smoothing iron.*

patentees were probably Dyer and Seely who were granted their patent on the 30th October 1883. (Fig 16).

EMBER IRONS. Alternative name for Charcoal Irons.

EYE IRONS. Charcoal irons with semi-circular openings in the sides of the body castings. Made from c.1870. (Fig 42).

FIRE BOX. The body casting of a charcoal iron.

FLOUNCE IRONS. See Sleeve and Flounce Irons.

FLUTERS. Irons or machines used for putting pleats into cloth. Inventors had various ideas on the form fluting machines should take. Some machines held the stacked material in place until it dried in the creases. Other types of machine included flat-bed boards with wooden slats pressed into place to form the pleats; devices with corrugated rollers that meshed into ridges on a board; others looked like wringers with teeth. (Fig 20, 33)

Scissor-like irons for putting flutes into material were introduced towards the close of the nineteenth century. These were also known as *quilling tongs.* (Fig 19)

Fluting attachments were also fitted to smoothing irons and most manufacturers listed some of these dual-purpose irons in their catalogues. (Fig 43)

GAS IRONS. Gas lighting was a practical reality in England as early as 1792 and 1820 in the U.S.A.

David Lithgow was granted a U.S. Patent covering the design for a gas iron in 1858 and, in his application, refers to previous inventions of a similar kind. It is reasonable to suppose that gas was the fuel for the first true self-heating irons. (Fig 11, 12)

GASOLINE IRONS. See Petrol Irons.

GNIDESTEIN (rubbing stone). The overall term for smooth round stones and glass balls used cold by Scandinavian women for smoothing cloth.

Glass balls and glass mushroom-shaped smoothers were still being made in the late eighteenth century. (Fig 3)

GOFFERING IRONS. Originated in the sixteenth century and intended to form ruffles and tucks in costume.

These irons were developed in Italy and in the early years of their appearance were known as *tally* (short for Italy) irons. They later acquired the name *goffering* irons from a corruption of the French word for the process. (Fig 18. 27-29)

GOOSE. See Tailors' and Laundry Irons.

HATTERS' IRONS. The hat-making and millinery trades in the eighteenth and nineteenth centuries called for, and were given by the iron manufacturers, a whole range of special irons in numerous shapes and sizes. (Fig 35, 36, 267-270)

HEATER IRONS. See Box Irons.

HEEL. The rear or blunt end of a smoothing iron.

ITALIAN IRONS. See Goffering Irons.

KEROSENE IRONS. See Paraffin Irons

LACE IRONS. Diminutive versions of home laundry irons. (Fig. 44).

LATCH. Device for fastening the gate on a box iron, and for holding down the lid of a charcoal iron to the fire box. The knob of the latch was often decorative, cast in the form of a human head or an animal, particularly on the charcoal irons made in Germany and Austria. The primary purpose of a knob was to give weight to the latch so the lid would close automatically.

LAUNDRY IRONS. See Tailors' and Laundry Irons.

LID. The hinged top-plate of a charcoal iron.

MANGLING BOARD. A Northern European device for smoothing cloth, probably devised in the sixteenth century. The board, often ornately carved and sometimes with a corrugated lower surface, was used with a plain wooden roller. (Fig 4, 5)

    Mangling boards were taken abroad by settlers, and were made and used in Indonesia, the U.S.A., and South Africa.

META IRONS. See Spirit Irons.

METHYLATED SPIRIT IRONS. See Spirit Irons.

MRS POTTS IRON. A detachable handled iron, pointed at both ends, patented in the U.S.A. by Mrs Mary Florence Potts in 1870, and made in a number of countries both under licence and after the patent expired.

    A set of Mrs Potts Irons comprised a handle and three bodies—two heating on the stove and one in use. (Fig 45, 163, 164).

NAPHTHA-HEATED IRONS. There was a U.S. Patent, granted in 1868, to a D. H. Lowe covering an iron heated by naphtha. This is an unusual heating agent and it is not known if the iron went into series production.

ORIENTAL PAN IRONS. Dating from the pre-eighth century period and a form still being used in Eastern countries. It is difficult to date these irons. Similar traditional decorations have been used for centuries and there have been many attempts at faking. The genuine antiques have hardwood handles, usually ornately carved, and handles of jade and ivory and not unknown. (Fig 46).

PAN IRONS. See Oriental Pan Irons above.

PARAFFIN IRONS. Paraffin (called Kerosene in the U.S.A.) heated irons started to be made in the 1890s.

PETROL IRONS. Petrol (called Gasoline in the U.S.A.) heated irons were made first in the later years of the nineteenth century, probably originating in the U.S.A. (Fig 60).

44

45

46

44   Lace iron with detachable handle.
45   A Kenrick (West Bromwich) built Mrs. Potts iron, made under licence from 1880.
46   Chinese silk iron—eighteenth century.

47

48

47   *Glazing or polishing iron.*
48   *Sad iron—nineteenth century. Probably*
     English.

POLISHING IRONS. It was fashionable during the latter half of the nineteenth century for starched garments to have a glazed appearance. This was achieved by rubbing hard with an iron which had a convex sole, a patterned sole or a rounded edge to the heel. (Fig 47).

QUILLING TONGS or **SCISSORS.** See Fluters.

ROTARY IRONERS. Ironing machines with revolving rollers are the logical development of the clothes wringer which, in turn, was inspired by the North European mangling boards. Rotary ironing was in laundry use in the early years of the twentieth century. (Fig 184).

SAD IRONS. An often misused term. Strictly, it should be applied only to solid-bodied irons which are heated on a stove. However, it is often used to describe box, charcoal and self-heating irons, particularly those of extra heavy weight. *Heavy* being a meaning of the word *sad*, as any housewife who has made a mess of cake making will confirm. (Fig 48).

SELF-HEATING IRONS. The author feels that this term should be applied to irons which have heat-generating fuel actually ignited within their bodies. It is, however, quite common to see the term used to cover charcoal irons for which the fuel is ignited outside the iron. It is of little importance providing all concerned are aware of the possible confusion.

SLEEVE AND FLOUNCE IRONS. Both the terms mean the same thing: an iron (usually a sad iron) with a long and narrow enough sole and body to reach into a pleat or up a sleeve. They are thought to have been evolved first in Europe in the 1830s. (Fig 140).

SLIKJIKJAKJE and **SLIKJITONNA** (meaning *jaw bone of a cow* and *tooth of a pig*). Early Scandinavian implements used for smoothing linen and embroidery.

SLUG IRONS. See Box Irons.

SMOKE STACK. A chimney provided on the lid of a charcoal iron.

SOAPSTONE IRONS. It is known that at least one manufacturer made bodies for sad irons from soapstone faced with steel soles. This was Phineas B. Hood of Milford, New Hampshire, who was granted a U.S. Patent in 1867. It was said that soapstone retained heat better than an all metal sad iron. (Fig 141).

SOLE. The base or rubbing serface of a smoothing iron.

SPIRIT IRONS. Spirit and alcohol irons that started to appear on the market in the 1850s were mainly intended for travellers, although some were for household use. Derivatives were the travelling irons using solidified methylated spirit (meta), which was burned outside the iron on a small stove on which the iron could be heated in an inverted position. (Fig 13).

STANDING IRONS. Special egg-, ball-, and mushroom-shaped irons were evolved in the early nineteenth century. They were either fixed on upright bases or hand held, and their purpose was to iron awkward shaped parts of a garment from the inside. Standing irons are still used today in laundries where they are combined with integral steam jets. (Fig 23-26).

STRAP HANDLE. Flat metal strip fabricated or bent to form the posts to handle grip. The strap handle is usually found on economy models whereas more expensive irons have cast posts.

SWISS STYLE. A term used by the Grossag company to describe a charcoal iron with a series of small holes around the lower part of the fire box casting to effect a draught for burning the charcoal. (Fig 50).

TAILORS' AND LAUNDRY IRONS. These are extra heavy irons of the sad (or solid) variety, as well as charcoal, gas or electrically heated. A particular type is the Tailor's Goose—an odd shape going back well into the seventeenth century. It is named after the shape of the handle which is simply a bar forming the post and bent forward in a curve like a goose's neck.

Tailors' irons usually range in weight from 16 to 22 pounds, although some weigh as much as 60 pounds. (Fig 51).

TALLY IRONS. See Goffering Irons.

'TATTLE-TALE' HANDLES. A means of knowing if the servant working on the ironing was slacking. The hollow handle contained a small bell which tinkled while the iron was in motion. This may sound a nasty petty spying device and one that could only have been used by our ancestors, but it must be remembered that cash registers still have a bell which rings when the drawer is opened to draw the attention of the shop-manager so he can see that the assistant is not taking out more than is put in. What a mistrusting lot we are!

TRAVELLING IRONS. Small, readily transportable irons intended for use in hotel and boarding house rooms. The fuel was generally methylated spirits but as electric irons became safer in the first few years of the twentieth century, a number of this type appeared on the market. Travelling irons often doubled as water heaters; reminders of the days when h & c running water was a rare luxury. (Fig 126).

TRIVET. A three-legged stand for a hot iron, usually made from cast iron but sometimes from brass. They are frequently very ornate.

WEASEL. An early nineteenth century slang term for a tailor's goose. See Tailors' and Laundry Irons.

WESTPHALIA or OX-TONGUE. A late nineteenth century style of box iron made by Grossag of Schwabisch-Hall, Germany, but copied by many other makers in Germany and Austria and in parts of France where the German influence was strong. (Fig 52).

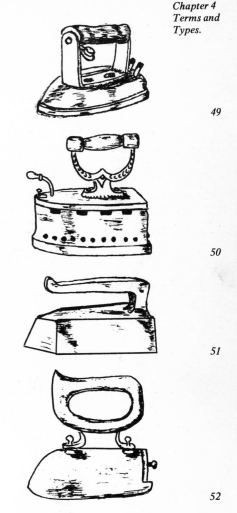

49

50

51

52

49   Typical 1930s strap handle electric iron with thumb rest.

50   'Swiss Form' iron by Grossag. 1920s.

51   Goose by Camion Freres. Early nineteenth century.

52   Westphalian form of box iron with U-type handle by Grossag.

53

54

55

53   Stuart cap iron.
54   Atkins hot-water iron.
55   Irons with their trivets. The trivet lower
      centre is a commemorative product on the
      occasion of Queen Victoria's Diamond
      Jubilee. Marked '60th year of H.M. reign'.

Chapter Five

DIRECTORY OF INVENTORS, MAKERS AND MARQUES.

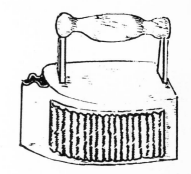

It cannot be claimed that the following list is a comprehensive survey of all the names connected with the long and complex history of the smoothing iron. Hitherto unknown makes are continually coming to light and even while the typescript for this book is being prepared additional information and corrections are being gathered by the author. However, the Directory will be useful to collectors when tracing histories of irons.

AAS GLASS WORKS. A Scandinavian factory making glass *slikjitonna* (glass balls for smoothing cloth). Active: 1748-64. (Fig 3).

ABBOTTS & COMPANY. A British foundry active at least in the 1850s.

A-BEST-O. A trade name of the Dover Mfg Co., of Dover, Ohio.

ACME. A marque of electric iron listed in the 1922 mail order catalogue of Butler Brothers in the U.S.A.

ACME SELF-HEATING IRON COMPANY. Ravenna, Ohio. Makers of the Acme Carbon Iron—a combination fluting and smoothing iron granted a U.S. Patent on Mar 15, 1910. (Fig 56, 57).

ADAMS COMPANY, Dubuque, Iowa.

ADAMS, F. C. (inventor). Granted U.S. Patent for a charcoal iron in 1852.

AETNA IRON COMPANY. 173 Railroad Avenue (same address as Bless & Drake), Newark, N.J. The Aetna self-heating iron was patented on Dec 17, 1907. Presumably Aetna and Bless & Drake were connected. (Fig 58).

AKRON LAMP AND MFG CO. Akron, Ohio. Founded c.1890 and active until 1947. Makers of the Diamond which was marketed under their own name, the Radiant, for the Radiant Products Company also of Akron; Maid of Honor for the Sears, Roebuck mail order company; Ward's Quick Lighting for Montgomery Ward—also a mail order company. All these were irons of identical design and could be used with either petrol or paraffin (gasoline or kerosene in the U.S.A.). The fuel tanks were orginally ball-shaped but were a streamlined form c.1937. (Fig 66).

56

57

58

56,57 'Acme' combination fluting and smoothing iron. c.1910.

58 Aetna. c.1908.

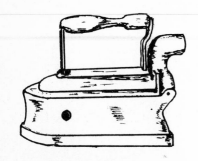

59

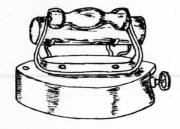

60

61

59   *Tailor's iron by Allerups, Denmark.*

60   *American Gas Company petrol iron.*
      c.1913.

61   *'Eagle' fluter.*

ALBRECHT, HERMAN. Philadelphia (inventor). Granted U.S. Patents on Nov 2, 1875 and reissued on Mar 23, 1880, covering a fluting maching made by North Brothers and called the Union.

ALLEN & COMPANY, W. T. SHERWOOD FOUNDRY, MANSFIELD, Nottingham. A foundry active at least in c.1880.

ALLERUPS, A/S M. P. Efterfolgere, Odense, Denmark. Maker of tailors' box irons. (Fig 59).

AMERICAN FOUNDRY AND MANUFACTURING COMPANY. An American maker of irons also known during their history as: the Etter Foundry, Etter & Henger Mfg Co, and Henger & Plueger.

AMERICAN GAS MACHINE COMPANY. Albert Lea, Minn.; Fargo, N.D.; Memphis, Tenn.; and New York City. Makers of petrol irons under the U.S. Patent granted to Hans C. Hanson in 1912. (Fig 60).

AMERICAN IRONING MACHINE COMPANY, Chicago, Ill. Agents for several iron manufacturers: The Simplex Electric Heating Company of Cambridge, Mass., the Joseph Gross Company of Milwaukee, Wisc., and the Imperial Brass Mfg Co. of Chicago, Ill.

AMERICAN MACHINE COMPANY, Philadelphia, Pa. There was a connection with the Enterprise Co., and probably with North Brothers. The American Machine Company made irons with the marques: Eagle, Union, Penn, American, Eclipse, and Star. They also made The Original Knox, a crimping machine patented by Susan R. Knox in April 1870 and July 1877. (Fig 61).

ANKER HEEGARD, Denmark. Took over the Frederike-vaerk foundry in 1848.

ARNOLD, G. B. With A. H. Price and A. S. Urner, granted U.S. Patent for self-heating goffering irons on July 24, 1860.

ASBESTOS. The trade name of the Dover Mfg Co., Dover, Ohio. Under this marque was marketed a skirted iron with a flip-over latch. (Fig 67, 68).

ASHBURY, T. H. With J. H. Baker, U.S. Patentee of the Patent Ground Star Iron.

ASHWORTH, Burnley, Lancs. A foundry active at least in the 1850s.

ASMUS, E. G. (inventor). Granted U.S. Patent covering a charcoal iron in 1891.

ATHERTON & COMPANY, A. Wolverhampton, England. Manufacturers of irons, the designs for which were registered in 1844. (Fig 69).

ATKINS. Maker of hot water irons.

AUER-GESELISCHAFT, Dresden, Germany. Believed to have marketed the Dalli charcoal/patent fuel iron in the 1928-30 period. The Dalli was made by the Grossag Company from at least 1911, when it was listed in Whiteley's of London catalogue. This was a similar iron to the Flott, produced by Carl Pack of Germany. (Fig 71).

AUTOMAT. The name given to a type of latch used on some charcoal irons made by Grossag in Germany.

BACHE, William. A prominent English smith who was active in the 1680s and who almost certainly made irons.

BAIRD & COMPANY, Pittsburgh, Pa. Makers of the Sweeney Iron, a polisher patented by Mary Sweeney in November 1896. (Fig 62).

62

BAKER, J. H. With T. H. Ashbury, the U.S. Patentee of the Patent Ground Star Iron.

BAKEWELL, Robert. Derby. A prominent English smith who was active in the early seventeenth century and who almost certainly made irons.

BARNES, Daniel A. Granted on December 11, 1877, a U.S. Patent covering an ornamental design for a sad iron. It was cast in the shape of a swan with a baby swan on its back.

BEHRSTOCK, L. 765 W. Van Buren Street, Chicago, Ill. Maker of the Gross Star electric tailor's iron c.1920. (Fig 63).

63

BELL, W. Granted U.S. Patent for a charcoal iron in 1889.

BERLINER INDUSTRIES, Germany. Made charcoal irons with the chimney in the shape of a monster's head. It is believed they were made in in the 1920s and '30s by this and other German companies.

BEST ON EARTH. A marque used in the U.S.A. for a Mrs Potts type iron after the expiration of the patent, the renewal of which was issued in 1880.

BISHOP, G. W. Granted U.S. Patent for a charcoal iron in 1856.

64

BLAYLOCK & COMPANY, John. Long Island Foundry, Carlisle. A foundry active at least in the 1850s.

BLESS & DRAKE, Newark, N.J. Active between 1856 and 1927, during which time it was one of the most important of smoothing iron manufacturing concerns. It was founded by Eleazer Bless and Robert Drake and the company remained as a family partnership through three generations. The trade mark of the company was Salamander.

62   *Sweeney. 1899.*

63   *Gross Star electric iron.*

64   *Bless & Drake's detachable-handle sad iron. Made from 1886.*

Chapter 5
Directory of
Inventors, Makers
and Marques.

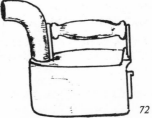

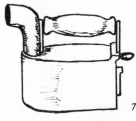

Apart from the irons invented by themselves, James Bless in particular, Bless & Drake manufactured the Taliferro & Cummings patent charcoal iron from the 1850s—this iron was still listed in 1930 and being produced at a rate of 100,000 per year.

The company made the Mrs Potts iron under licence until the patent expired and then continued with some improvements of their own patents: Dec 7, 1886 and May 6, 1889.

One of the more interesting of the irons made by Bless and Drake was a charcoal box tailor's iron of the same design as one made by J. & J. Siddons of West Bromwich, England. Examples from both foundries carried the head of Hephaestus, the Greek patron of iron-workers.

Sleeve irons, bearing the patent date of 1897 were made as premium gifts for the Grand Union Tea Company.

There may have been a connection between Bless & Drake in the U.S.A. and J. & J. Siddons in England, and there was certainly a connection with the Aetna Sad Iron Company who shared the address of 175 Railroad Avenue, Newark, N.J. (Fig 64, 65, 72, 73).

B. o O. LIBERGSF, A. B. A Norwegian foundry making irons at least in the late nineteenth century. (Fig 74).

BONUS. A petrol iron made by Archibald Kenrick & Sons Limited of West Bromwich.

BRADFORD, Thomas. Crescent Iron Works, Salford, Manchester. Active at least in the 1870s.

BRILLIANT. A spirit iron patented by Josef Feldmeyer of Wurzburg, Germany. Patents were also issued in Austria, Belgium, France, Italy, Great Britain and the U.S.A. and manufactured in most of these countries apart from Germany. All the patents were issued around the year 1897. (Fig 13).

BRITANNIA MANUFACTURING COMPANY, Colchester, Essex. Active at least in the 1860s.

BRODIE, G. G. See Eagle Range & Foundry Company.

BROWN, Jeremiah W. Hartford, Conn. Granted a U.S. Patent covering a spirit iron on Mar 21, 1854. This was a reversible iron—the top plate was heating while the lower plate was in use as a sole. (Fig 84).

BROWN, John P. (inventor). Granted U.S. Patent covering an improved handle on May 19, 1896. The manufacture was assigned to the Enterprise company.

BROWN & FOSTER, Mount Morris, New York. Makers of tailors' box irons. (Fig 76).

74

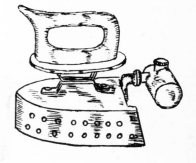

75

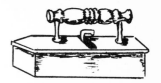

76

74   *Box iron by B o O Libersf, Norway. Late nineteenth century.*

75   *'Brilliant' spirit iron designed by Josef Feldmeyer.*

76   *Box iron by Brown and Foster.*

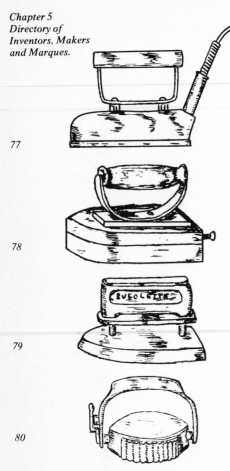

77

78

79

80

77   B.T.H. English made iron. c.1910.

78   Westphal's 'Buffalo' gas iron. The heat
      escape ports are drilled in the right-hand
      side of the iron, away from the operator.

79   'Bugolette' solidified methylated spirit
      (meta) travelling iron.

80   'Ladies' Friend' combined fluting and
      smoothing iron. c.1900. There was a
      similar iron called the 'O.K. Family
      Iron', with a polishing edge in place of
      the fluter.

BROWN MANUFACTURING COMPANY, Cincinnati, Ohio. Makers of the Standard spirit iron.

BRUNCKER, George. A prominent English smith who was active in the late seventeenth and early eighteenth centuries and who almost certainly made irons.

B.T.H. An electric iron marketed in England in 1911. (Fig 77).

BUFFALO. A gas iron invented by Charles H. Westphal in 1877 and made by the Buffalo Forge Company, Buffalo, New York. (Fig 78).

BUGOLETTE. A German made travelling iron burning solidified methylated spirit cubes. (Fig 79).

BUNTING-STONE COMPANY, Kansas City.

BURNOT. A marque used by William Cross & Company of West Bromwich who were active between 1835 and 1940. There were several variations: The Burnot Patent Fuel Iron, and the Baby Burnot.

BUTLER BROTHERS. An American wholesale mail order company whose catalogue was called 'Our Brummer'.

BUTT, John M. Gloucester. An iron foundry active at least in the 1850s.

CAIFFA, Le. The marque of a premium gift iron distributed by a coffee marketing company between 1910 and 1940. There is carried a pictorial mark of an old man with a bottle of wine in one hand and a pipe in the other. Of similar form to Le Parisien Iron. (Fig 85).

CAMION FRERES, Vivier-au-Court, France. Founded in 1820 and still active. The trade mark is an anchor. Irons have been made under various trade names: Demi-Fortes, Renforces, du Midi, Moraimont, Algeriens, and Alsaciens. (Fig 51, 86, 87).

CAMPBELL, George J. Philadelphia, Pa. Maker of the Verebest gas iron.

CAMPO. A trade mark found on a charcoal iron made by the Cannon Company Limited of Bilston, Staffs. Probably a special order.

CANAL DOVER MANUFACTURING COMPANY. See Dover Mfg Co.

CANNON COMPANY LIMITED, Bilston, Staffs. Tradesmark has, at times, been a cannon. Founded in 1826, the foundry made irons up to 1900. (Fig 88, 89, 90).

CAROLINA. A marque used by Archibald Kenrick & Sons Limited on Charcoal irons.

CARRON COMPANY. Mungal Foundry, Carron, Near Falkirk.

CARVER, Horace P. Racine, Wisc. Granted a U.S. Patent Jan 3, 1899, covering a reversible iron. Under this patent Carver made the O.K. Family Laundry Iron, Ladies' Friend, The Victor, and The Economist. (Fig 80).

CHALFANT MANUFACTURING COMPANY, Issac P. Arglen and Philadelphia, Pa. Made the Mrs Potts Iron under licence.

CHARMA. A marque used by William Cross & Company, West Bromwich, for a series of charcoal irons. (Fig 81).

CHRISTENSEN, N. A. Nykjobing, Denmark. A foundry active at least c.1900. (Fig 82).

CLARK, L. D. Stoughton, Wisc. (inventor). With O. Tverdahl, granted U.S. Patent for an asbestos insulated iron on May 22, 1900. The iron was made by the Dover Mfg Co., Dover, Ohio. (Fig 68, 91).

CLARK, T. & C. An English foundry active in 1888 when an iron manufacturers' association was formed. (Fig 83).

CLARK'S WARRANTED CRIMPING MACHINE, Thomas. An English built crimping machine probably produced by T. & C. Clark. (Fig 22).

CLAYTON, Herbert. New York. Granted U.S. Patents of July 4, 1893 and Dec 4, 1900 covering a combined lamp and iron, burning either coal (natural in U.S.A.) gas or alcohol. Sold as the Sultana Toilet Iron. (Fig 93).

CLEVELAND FOUNDRY, Cleveland, Ohio.

COALBURN, George. A prominent English smith who was active in the late seventeenth and early eighteenth centuries and who almost certainly made irons.

COCHRANE & COMPANY, Woodside Iron Works, Dudley, England. Active at least in the 1850-70 period.

COLEBROOKDALE IRON FOUNDRY. Boyertown, and Pottstown, Pa. Started making irons in 1852. A diamond trademark was used c.1892, but they also used a shield, a star, a box, and a keystone at other times. The foundry produced the Mrs Potts iron until 1953 and were probably the last in the U.S.A. to make it. (Fig 92).

COLEMAN COMPANY, Wichita, Kansas. Made the Sunshine petrol iron under the patents of John E. McCutchen and Boyd W. Tullis and in 1925 produced the iron under their own name of Coleman. Model 2 appeared in 1925, Model 8A in 1930, Model 4A in 1940, and 609 in 1940. (Fig 94).

COLT COMPANY, J. B. Chicago, Kansas City, and San Francisco. This is not the firearms manufacturer but a maker of carbide-acetylene appliances, including irons, from the early years of the twentieth century. (Fig 37).

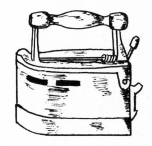

81

82

83

81   *'Charma' by William Cross.*

82   *Christensen, Denmark. c.1900.*

83   *Sad iron by T & C Clark. c.1910.*

Chapter 5
Directory of
Inventors, Makers
and Marques.

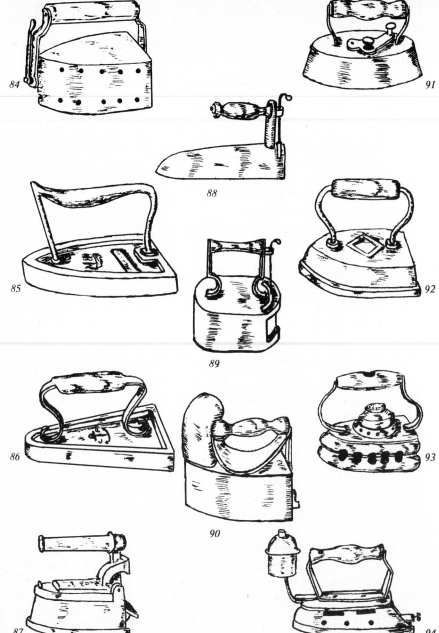

84   Reversible spirit iron by the Rotary Smoothing Iron Company, U.S.A. Patented 1854.

85   French sad iron c.1880—Le Parisien.

86   French sad iron by Camion Freres. Mid-nineteenth century.

87   Charcoal iron by Camion Freres.

88   'French Pattern' box iron by Cannon. c.1835.

89   'Dutch Pattern' box iron by Cannon. c. 1835.

90   A Cannon charcoal iron. Very similar styles were made by J & J Siddons, Archibald Kenrick, and George Salter.

91   Dover 'skirted' iron c.1895. The heater slug, carried under the skirt, is released by the latch.

92   Colebrookdale. c.1892.

93   'Sultana' Toilet Iron. Apart from use with its own burner it can also be heated over a gas jet.

94   Coleman Model 2 1925. Earlier 'Sunshine' models made by this company had vertically cylindrical tanks.

COMFORT. An alcohol iron patented in September 1903 and made by the Hawkes Flat-Iron Company, Chicago, Ill. A prominent feature of the iron is its very large cast-aluminium tank. (Fig 95).

COMFORT. A petrol iron made by the National Stamping and Electric Works, Chicago, Ill. (Fig 96).

COMPANION. An American marque of clamp-on-the-table fluter. (Fig 97).

COOK, Mary Ann B. Boston, Mass. (inventor). Granted U.S. Patent covering a polishing iron with a convex sole on Dec 5, 1848. (Fig 36).

CORRISTER, W. D. With Susan R. Knox, granted U.S. Patent in April 1866 covering a crimping machine.

COSBY, E. B. Granted a U.S. Patent on Oct 23, 1888, covering the design of a sad iron in the shape of a railway locomotive. (Fig 38).

COSCO PRODUCTS CORPORATION. In the 1920s this concern produced an electric neck-tie ironer called the Press Rite.

COTTINGHAM, G. Granted U.S. Patent for a charcoal iron in 1875.

COWING & COMPANY, Seneca Falls, New York. A maker of irons who had ceased to be active by 1875. (Fig 98).

CRANE & COMPANY, C. H. Wolverhampton, Staffs. Their charcoal irons are of similar design to those of the Cannon company.

CRANE & COMPANY, W. M. New York City.

CROSS & SON LIMITED, William. West Bromwich, Staffs. The company was founded in 1835 and still making irons up to 1940. Marques included: Hot Cross, Otto, Charma, Workwell, Burnot, Tozot, and Lyng. (Fig 99).

Hot Cross gas irons were made under patents granted to Cross and Kirby. (Fig 107).

The Mrs Potts iron was produced under the Tozot label. (Fig 108).

CROWN. A fluting machine made by North Brothers of Philadelphia. Some models of the Crown carried patent dates Nov 2, 1875, Jul 3, 1877 and a reissue date of Mar 23, 1880. The first and last patents were granted to Herman Albrecht of Philadelphia. (Fig 109).

CROWN JEWEL. A crimping machine made by Lowerre & Tucker, Newark, N.J., under the patent of Henry C. Sergeant, on Nov 23, 1869.

CUMMINGS, William. See Taliferro & Cummings.

DALLI. A charcoal burning iron made by the Grossag company in Germany. An alternative patent fuel was also offered. It was certainly made in 1911 when it was listed in Whiteley's of London catalogue and probably for some time before. In the 1928-30 period it is thought to have been made for the Auer-Gesellschaft concern of Dresden. The Dalli bears a striking

95

96

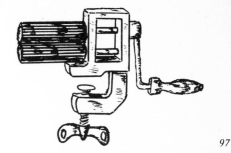

97

95 'Comfort' alcohol iron. c.1904.

96 'Comfort'.

97 'Companion' fluter.

Chapter 5
Directory of
Inventors, Makers
and Marques.

98   *Cowing. c.1870.*

99   *'LYNG' by William Cross & Sons Limited. The hollow handle is an English characteristic.*

100   *A polishing iron by William Cross.*

101   *The 'Darwin' shape by William Cross & Sons Ltd.*

102   *'Lyng' box iron by William Cross.*

103   *Box iron by William Cross. The design is based on the 1738 patent of Isaac Wilkinson.*

104   *'Lyng' iron by William Cross.*

105   *Tailor's iron by William Cross. The style, incorporating the handle twists, was produced by many manufacturers.*

106   *Gas iron by William Cross.*

107   *'Hot Cross' made by William Cross & Sons Ltd.*

108   *'Tozot' detachable handle box iron by William Cross.*

109   *'Crown' fluting machine.*

102
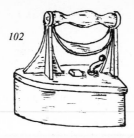

106

103
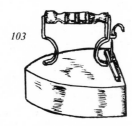

107

104
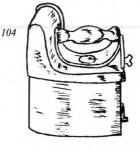

108

98

100

99
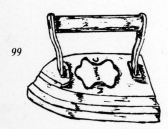

101

105
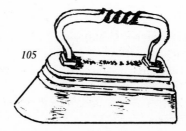

109
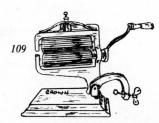

resemblance to the Flott iron built by Carl Pack Company also of Germany.

DARWIN SAD IRON. Catalogued by Thomas Shelden & Company Limited in 1920. Darwin irons were also made by the William Cross foundry in West Bromwich. (Fig 101, 110)

DIAMOND. A petrol iron made by the Akron Lamp & Mfg Co., Akron, Ohio. (Fig 66).

DIETZ, J. B. Granted U.S. Patent on Dec 5, 1882 covering a tailor's iron, which comprised a heated roller held in an insulated handle.

DOVER MANUFACTURING COMPANY, Dover, Ohio. Sometimes called The Canal Dover Mfg Co. Marques included Dover—a skirted iron with a single centre post for a latch, A-Best-O, and Asbestos—irons made under U.S. Patent of May 22, 1900, granted to O. Tverdahl and L. D. Clark of Stoughton, Wisc. (Fig 67, 68, 91).

DOWNS & COMPANY, Senaca Falls, New York. 1856 was the year this maker started to produce irons—the factory being founded in 1840 as pump manufacturers. In 1869 the name was changed to the Gould Mfg Co., but production of the Downs iron continued until 1881. (Fig 111).

DRAKE, Robert. See Bless & Drake.

DURETTE. An Austrian made solidified methylated spirit travelling iron. (Fig 112).

DYER, Richard N. Collaborated with Henry W. Seely for the U.S. Patent of Oct 30, 1883, covering an electric iron. (Fig 16).

DYER & SONS, Southampton, England. A foundry active at least in the 1890s.

EAGLE. A fluting machine made by the American Machine Company of Philadelphia, Pa. (Fig 61).

EAGLE RANGE & FOUNDRY COMPANY. Eagle Foundry, Broad Street, Birmingham, England. Active at least in the 1870s and '80s.

ECLIPSE. A fluting machine made by the American Machine Company, Philadelphia, Pa.

ECLIPSE. An American made box iron patented Aug 25, 1903.

ECONOMICA. A Spanish made charcoal iron.

ECONOMIST, The. See Horace P. Carver.

EDMUNDS, John M. Salt Lake City. Granted a U.S. Patent Apr 18, 1882, covering a water-heated-by-spirit iron. (Fig 117).

EDNA. Marque of charcoal iron, probably used by J. & J. Siddons or George Salter.

110

111

112

110 A 'Darwin' shape by Thomas Sheldon & Company Limited.

111 Sad iron by Downs & Company. c.1860-1880.

112 'Durette' solidified methylated spirit travelling iron.

113

114

115

EDNEY, William, Bristol, England. A prominent smith who was active in the late seventeenth and early eighteenth centuries, and who almost certainly made irons.

ELB, Max. Dresden, Germany. Produced a patented charcoal iron in Germany. He was granted a U.S. Patent on Dec 7, 1899. (Fig 113).

ELEGANT. A marque used by the Grossag company in Germany. (Fig 114).

EMERSON MANUFACTURING COMPANY, Los Angeles, California. Maker of box irons. (Fig 115).

ENTERPRISE MANUFACTURING COMPANY, Philadelphia, Pa. Founded in 1866. In 1955 the company was absorbed by the Procter-Silex Corporation. There was a connection between Enterprise and the American Machine Co. A very important maker of irons, Enterprise made numerous types: the Ground Star under patents granted on Oct 1, 1867 Jan 16, 1877, the Mrs Potts Patent Iron, the iron patented by Charles F. Mosher in December 1900, handles patented by John W. Brown on May 19, 1896, and the Star Polishing Iron, sometimes referred to as the Chinese Polisher, patented in 1877 and catalogued until 1915. (Fig 118).

Enterprise irons were made under licence by the Frederiks-Vaerk foundry in Denmark.

ETTER FOUNDRY. This American concern had some name changes including Etter & Henger Mfg Co., Henger & Plueger, and American Foundry & Mfg Co.

EVANS, H. B. Granted a U.S. Patent covering charcoal irons in 1876.

EVER READY. An American box iron patented on Feb 6, 1917. (Fig 119).

FAGOEL. A Mexican made charcoal iron marked with the date Jan 3, 1957. (Fig 120).

FAY, James J. Worcester, Mass. With David A. Upham, granted a patent for a gas iron to be made by the Worcester Gas Iron Company, Portland, from c.1889.

FELDMEYER, Josef. Worzburg, Germany. Patentee of the Brilliant spirit iron. (Fig 75).

FERROSTEEL COMPANY, Cleveland, Ohio.

FINN, George. Newark, N.J. Granted patent for a coke burning sad iron in 1902. This was marketed under the marque Ne Plus Ultra, by the National Iron Distributing Company, Drixel Hills, Pa. (Fig 121, 122).

FINNIGA, Manchester and Liverpool. Make of a spirit lamp-heated travelling iron.

FLOTT. A charcoal iron made in the early twentieth century by Carl Pack, Erkrath, Germany.

FOURNIER, F.N. Granted U.S. Patent for a charcoal iron in 1896.

FOX SAD IRON COMPANY, New York City.

113   Max Elb, Dresden. c.1898.

114   'Elegant' iron by Grossag. 1920s.

115   Emerson.

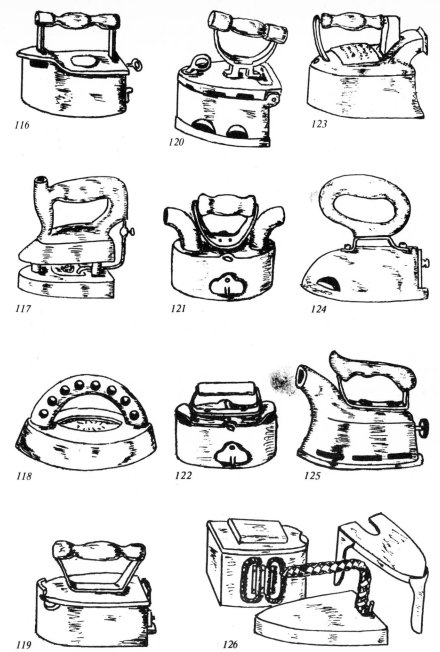

116

120

123

117

121

124

118

122

125

119

126

116   Eclipse. c.1904.

117   Edmund's hot-water iron. 1882. The spirit
       lamp heats the water in the upper chamber
       which then flows into the base.

118   Patent Ground Star Iron by Enterprise.
       1877.

119   Ever Ready. 1917.

120   'Fagoel'. A Mexican iron. Modern.

121   Ne Plus Ultra by George Finn. 1902.

122   Ne Plus Ultra by George Finn. 1916.

123   Gaillet charcoal iron.

124   'Gebe' box iron made in Austria. The
       name suggests it was made for the British
       market (G.B.—Great Britain).

125   'Ge-Mo' made by the General Motors
       factory in Denmark. 1930s.

126   G.E.C. Magnet travelling iron. c.1920.

Chapter 5
Directory of
Inventors, Makers
and Marques.

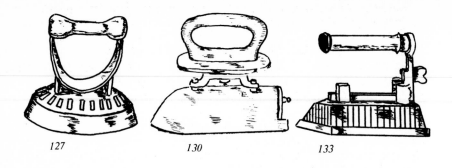

127   130   133

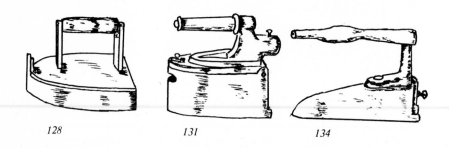

128   131   134

127   Gleason Cold-Handle Iron. 1870.

128   Goodwin box iron. Made in the U.S.A.
      1868.

129   Grall Polishing Iron. 1900.

130   'Westphalian' with 'R-Type' handle is the
      description given to this box iron by
      Grossag, the makers.

131   'French Form' iron by Grossag. 1920s.

132   'German Form' iron by Grossag. 1920s.

133   Sad iron goose by Grossag.

134   Box iron 'Berliner Form' goose by
      Grossag.

135   Charcoal iron by Grossag. 1920s.

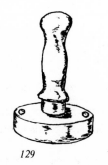
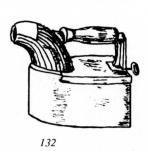
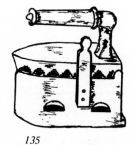

129   132   135

FREDERIKS-VAERK, Denmark. Founded in 1756, under the master, H. Hornbaver, and remained under his control until 1774. The foundry was bought by Anker Heegard in 1848. In its time the foundry has produced cannons and other military supplies and heavy castings. Enterprise irons were made here under licence. In 1875, they listed what they termed Franske Strygejern and Amerikanske Strygejern. (Fig 136).

FULUSE. British-made travelling iron using solidified methylated spirit. Available in the 1930s. (Fig 137).

FUNDICAU, Compannia Industrial. Porto, Portugal. Makers of charcoal irons. Still active. (Fig 138).

GAILLET, Paris. Maker of tailors' charcoal irons. (Fig 123).

GEBE. A marque of Austrian made box iron. (Fig 124).

GE-MO. Denmark. A marque of iron made by the Danish factory of General Motors c.1930, until 1940. (Fig 125).

GENERAL ELECTRIC. Made electric irons from c.1905. Their trade mark was, and is, Magnet.

GENEVA HAND FLUTER. Later models marketed as the Geneva Improved Fluter. Made from 1866 to at least 1920 by W. H. Howell, Geneva, Ill., to the design patented on Aug 21, 1866, by C. A. Sterling. (Fig 21).

GERMANIA. The name given to a style of one of their charcoal irons by Grossag. This was a square-sided and diamond-pointed body casting, more often thought to be a Swiss characteristic. (Fig 249).

GLEASON, Joel. Whitesone and Brooklyn, N.Y. Granted U.S. Patents on Jan. 22, 1870, July 12, 1870, and Sep 2, 1873. A feature of Gleason's iron was its handle which was designed for use without an iron-holder. (Fig. 127).

GOODWIN, Dr. Richard J.P. Manchester, N.H. Granted U.S. Patent for a box iron on Mar 3. 1868. (Fig 128).

GOULD MANUFACTURING COMPANY, Beneca Falls, N.Y. This is the name to which Downs & Co. was changed in 1869. Continued to make the Downs iron until 1881. (Fig 111).

GRAHAM & HAINES, U.S.A. Issued catalogue in 1881.

GRALL, J. G. Granted U.S. Patent for a polishing iron on Sep 4, 1900. (Fig 129).

GRAY, J. Granted U.S. Patent for a charcoal iron in 1868.

GREENWOOD & COMPANY, M. Cincinnati, U.S.A.

GRISSELL, H. & M. D. Regents Canal Iron Works, Eagle Wharf Road, Hoxton, London. Active at least in the 1850s.

GROSS, Joseph. Wilwaukee, Wisc. A coal (natural in U.S.A.) gas iron patented in 1898 was made by Gross and sold by the American Ironing Machine Company, Chicago.

GROSSAG, Schwabisch-Hall, Germany. One of the great names in smoothing iron making. The company was founded in 1863 and is still active. Grossag have made irons of many styles including that of the Mrs. Potts

136

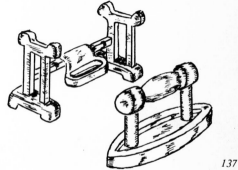

137

138

136 *'American Style' iron by Frederiks-vaerk. 1875.*

137 *'Fuluse' solidified methylated spirit travelling iron.*

138 *Charcoal iron by Companhia Industrial de Fundicau, Portugal. Modern.*

139 Only Base Burner by Wm. E. Hoyt (design by Thomas F. Hagerty). 1896.

140 Harper's flounce iron. A similar design is called 'Our Very Best'.

141 Hood soapstone sad iron. 1867.

iron which they called the American Style. One of their most famous irons was the Dalli, designed for use with charcoal or patent fuel, which was in production for many years. (Fig 71, 114, 130, 131, 132, 133, 134, 135).

GROSS STAR. An electric tailor's iron made by L. Behrstock, Chicago, Ill. (Fig 63).

GUIBERT, Boulogne, Seine, France. Maker of sad irons.

HAGERTY, T. F. San Francisco, Cali. Granted U.S. Patent on Mar 17, 1896, covering a charcoal iron called the Only Base Burner. The iron was made by William E. Hoyt of New York, who improved on the patent in 1898. (Fig 139).

HANDYSIDE & COMPANY, Britannia Foundry and Engineering Works, Derby, England. Active at least in the 1850s. The name was changed to Derby Castings Limited in 1931.

HANSON, Hans C. Albert Lea, Minn. Granted a U.S. Patent covering a petrol iron in 1912, which was manufactured by the American Gas Machine Company.

HARPERS, Chicago. Marketed a flounce iron with the patent date shown as Aug 27, 1907. (Fig 140).

HASS, C. J. Granted U.S. Patent for a charcoal iron in 1884.

HASSENRITTER, R. Granted U.S. Patent for a charcoal iron in 1875.

HAWKES FLAT IRON COMPANY, Chicago, Ill. Makers of the Comfort alcohol iron patented Sep 1903. (Fig 95).

HERBULOT, C. A. French manufacturer of sad irons in the nineteenth century.

HECHT, Ansel. New York City. Produced a fluter in April 1875 which could crimp material after it had been sewn into a garment.

HENGER & PLUEGER. See Etter Foundry.

HEWITT, John. New York City, later at Albany, and then Pittsburgh. Granted U.S. Patent on Mar 4, 1873, covering a fluting machine. This was one of eight patents issued to Hewitt in 1873 concerned with irons.

HOOD, Phineas E. Milford, N.H. Granted U.S. Patent on Jan 15, 1867 covering a sad iron with the body made from soapstone which was claimed to have better heat-retaining qualities than iron. (Fig 141).

HORNHAVER, H. The master of the Frederiks-vaerk foundry in Denmark, 1756-74.

HOT CROSS. A marque used by William Cross & Co. of West Bromwich, active 1835-1940. (Fig 107).

HOWELL, W. H. Geneva, Ill. Made irons of many designs, including the Geneva Hand Fluter (patented 1866) from 1866 to at least 1920. The emblem was a five-pointed star. (Fig 148).

HOYT, William E. New York. Maker of an iron based on T. F. Hagerty's patent. Hoyt improved on the patent in 1898. (Fig 139).

HUBBELL, Arthur Y. (inventor). See Patent Ground Star Iron.

HURDAL GLASS WORKS. Scandinavian maker of *slikjitonna*. Active up to 1783. (Fig 3).

IDEAL. An American made charcoal iron. According to the marks, the patent was applied for in 1905. (Fig 142).

IDEAL COMPANY. Springfield, Ohio. Makers of an alcohol iron, patented July 4, 1911. (Fig 143).

IDEAL SELF-HEATING FLAT IRON. A spirit iron made by the Worcester (Mass.) Self-Heating Flat Iron Co. c.1890. (Fig 144).

IMPERIAL GASOLINE IRON. A petrol iron patented in 1911 and made by the Imperial Brass Mfg Co., Chicago, for sale by the American Ironing Machine Co., also of Chicago. (Fig 149).

INTERNATIONAL. A petrol iron made by the National Stamping & Electric Works, Chicago, Ill.

IZONS & COMPANY. An English iron manufacturer. Active 1760-1914.

JENS, Maren. A Danish iron founder active in the 1660s.

JOHNSON, J. J. Granted U.S. Patent covering a charcoal iron in 1854.

JUBILEE. A spirit iron made in Omaha, Nebraska. Patented in 1899 and improved in 1904. (Fig 150).

KALLMAN, L. 974 Grand Street, N.Y. Made a polishing iron with a leather-grained pattern on the sole. Patterned soles were patented by Michael Mahony of Troy, N.Y.

KALTSCHMIDT, Karl, Oberriexingen, Germany. Product mark: 'K'. Makers of a tailors' iron with a detachable handle in the late nineteenth century—the style was still in production in the 1950s. (Fig 42, 151).

KENRICK. West Bromwich, Staffordshire. This founder made irons from 1791 and have since changed their name-style several times;
    From 1820—Archibald Kenrick & Company.
    From 1828—Archibald Kenrick & Son.
    From 1830—Archibald Kenrick & Sons.
    From 1883—Archibald Kenrick & Sons Limited.
Their 1835 catalogue lists Italian, Puffing, Egg, Mushroom, Ball, Frill, French, Flounce, German, Charcoal Box, Fluting, Sleeve and Piping Irons. By 1873 there were 35 types of irons in their range, each type in several sizes. Kenrick made the Mrs. Potts iron under licence from 1880, calling it the Mrs. Potts Patent Cold-Handle Sad Iron. The first Kenrick electric iron was made in 1912, and their G.L.C. Gas Iron was developed in 1935 with the collaboration of the Gas Light & Coke Company of London. Trade names: Carolina, and for petrol irons, Bonus. (Page 14. Fig 45, 152, 153, 154, 155, 156).

K.H.T. Hickory, U.S.A. Made the Mrs. Potts iron after the patent had expired.

KIMBALL & MORTON LIMITED, Glasgow. Active in the early twentieth century.

142

143

144

142 *Ideal. 1905.*

143 *'Ideal' alcohol iron. 1911.*

144 *'Ideal'. 1890.*

145

146

147

145 *Knapp-Monarch circular electric iron. 1930s.*

146 *Knapp combination fluting and smoothing iron. 1870. A similar iron was patented by Frederick Myers of New York.*

147 *Kuguenin charcoal iron. c.1890.*

KNAPP, Myron H. Bay City, Mich. Granted U.S. Patent on Aug 2, 1870 covering a combined fluting and smoothing iron. (Fig 146).

KNAPP-MONARCH, St. Louis, Mo. Made a round-soled electric iron in the 1930s. (Fig 145).

KNAUER, D. F. Pittsburgh, Pa. With William Warwick, patentee of irons marked 'F.K.'—sometimes appearing as 'E.K.' Active c.1860s.

KNOX, Susan R. (inventor). Original U.S. Patent granted in conjunction with W. D. Corrister in April 1866, covering a crimping machine. Further patent issued on Nov 20th, 1866 and the machine was produced by Henry Sauerbier & Son. Newark, N.J.

KUGUENIN, L. Fer Francais, Paris. Made a tailor's box iron in a style that changed little from 1890 to 1960. (Fig 147).

LADIES FRIEND. See Horace P. Carver. (Fig 80).

LAIDLOW & SONS, Alliance Foundry, Glasgow. Active at least in the 1850s.

LAKE, Bertus A. Big Prairie, Ohio. Maker of Monitor alcohol and spirit irons from the early years of the twentieth century. (Fig 157).

LAMB. A petrol iron made in South Sioux City, Nebraska. Patented in 1901 and improved in 1903. (Fig 158).

LANDERS, FRARY & CLARK. New Britain, Conn. Makers of the Universal Thermo-Cell iron—patented June 13, 1911—a similar style to the Potts iron. The company later made electric irons. (Fig 159).

LAUNDRY MAID. Marque of petrol irons made by the National Stamping & Electric Works, Chicago, Ill.

LEIGH, I. & W. Market Street, Manchester, England. Active at least in the 1850s.

LINK & MAHONY, Troy, N.Y. A partnership between Calvin W. Link and Michael Mahony. Active 1870-78.

LION FOUNDRY COMPANY LIMITED, Kirkintilloch, Glasgow. Active at least in the early twentieth century.

LITHGOW, David. Philadelphia. Granted a U.S. Patent covering a gas-heated iron on Oct 26, 1858. The iron was also made in Denmark. (Fig 11).

LOWE, D. H. Granted U.S. Patent for a Naphtha-heated iron on Nov 24, 1868.

LOWERRE & TUCKER, Newark, N.J. Makers of the Crown Jewel crimping machine, the patent for which was granted to Henry C. Sergeant on Nov 23, 1869.

LUDLOW, James. Albion Street, Birmingham, England. Active at least from the 1880s.

LYNG. A marque used by William Cross & Company of West Bromwich. It was applied to several types of iron. (Fig 99, 102, 104).

McCOY. An American made polishing iron.

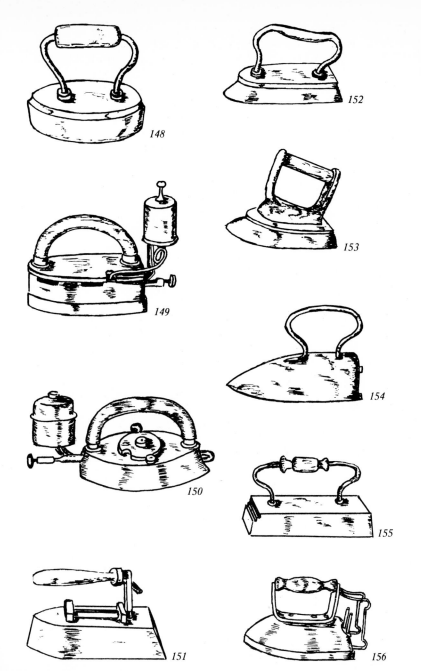

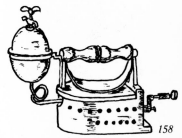

148 Howell Polishing Iron.

149 'Imperial' 1911.

150 'Jubilee' alcohol iron. 1899.

151 Sad iron goose by Kaltschmidt. Late nineteenth century.

152, Examples of Kenrick designed sad irons
153 made from the 1880s.

154 'German Pattern' box iron by Archibald Kenrick. 1880s.

155 Billiard table iron by Kenrick. Early 1920s.

156 Kenrick electric iron. 1920s.

157 'Monitor'. 1903.

158 'Lamb'. 1900.

159 Universal Therm-Cell. 1911.

160

161

162

McCUTCHEN, John E. An American patentee of an oil-burner assigned to the Coleman Company.

McDOWELL, STEVEN & COMPANY, Milton Iron Works, Glasgow, and Lauriston Iron Works, Falkirk. Active at least from the early twentieth century.

MAGIC. An American marque of box iron made in the 1870s.

MAGNET. Trade mark used by the General Electric Company.

MAHONY, Fred. Troy, N.Y. Fred and Michael Mahony carried on an iron making business from 1878 until the latter's death in 1899. Fred continued until 1918. See also Link & Mahony.

MAHONY, Michael. Troy, N.Y. Granted U.S. Patent for patterned sole in November 1878. A polishing iron under this patent was made by L. Kallman, N.Y. Mahony was active 1870-78 with Calvin W. Link, under name of Link & Mahony. After 1878 business was carried on with Michael in partnership with his brother, Fred. Michael Mahony died in 1899, the business being continued until 1918. (Fig 160).

MAID OF HONOR. A petrol iron made by the Akron Lamp and Mfg. Co., Akron, Ohio for the mail order concern of Sears, Roebuck & Company.

MAST, J. B. New York. Made hatters' irons in the nineteenth century using the marque 'JBM'. (Fig 161).

META FUEL IRON. A Swiss-made travelling iron heated by solidified methylated spirit cubes.

MEYER, E. L. Hildesheim, Germany. Makers of *ruffeleisen* or goffering irons, catalogued in 1887.

MODERN MANUFACTURING COMPANY. Orange, Calif. Makers of electrical irons from c.1909. (Fig 162).

MODERN SPECIALITY COMPANY. Milwaukee, Wisc. Made and/or marketed the Modern Alcohol Iron, patented Oct 19, 1909. The same castings were used on an iron made by the Sun Mfg. Co.

MONITOR. Alcohol and petrol irons made by Bertus A. Lake, Big Prairie, Ohio, under patent granted to him in the early twentieth century.

MOORE, W. B. Dublin and Cork. Active at least in the 1860s.

MOSHER, Charles P. Granted U.S. Patent in December 1900 covering a stand to enable the iron to lay on its side. Production was undertaken by the Enterprise foundry.

MRS. POTTS PATENT IRON. Mrs. Mary Florence Potts of Ottumwa, Iowa, was granted U.S. Patents covering a double-pointed iron, a circular detachable-handle, and non-conducting material between the base and the top-plate. The patents were assigned to the Chalfant foundry and later to the Enterprise Mfg. Co., and the American Machine Co. Some Enterprise Potts irons show a patent date of 1867 but the earliest found Mrs. Potts patent is May 24, 1870. There were several reissues, the latest being Jan 6, 1880. The franchise in Britain was held by Kenrick, who called the design

160   Mahony. 1876.

161   Hatter's 'shell' by J. B. Mast. Late nineteenth century.

162   'Modern'. 1909.

Mrs. Potts Patent Cold Handle Sad Iron. In Germany the iron was made by Grossag who gave it the name of American Style.

When the patent expired the iron was made by numerous manufacturers in the U.S.A., Germany, Denmark, Britain and Canada. (Fig 163, 164).

MRS. STREETER'S GEM POLISHER. A combined smoothing and polishing iron made by N. R. Streeter, Groton, New York. (Fig 165).

MURDOCH, G. J. Granted U.S. Patent on Mar 20, 1888, covering an iron with a thermostat that activated a bell when cooling. No evidence that the iron was produced.

MYERS, Frederick, New York. Granted ten U.S. Patents between March 1871 and March 1873. These included one on Sep 17, 1872 covering a gas burner over which the iron was placed in an inverted position for heating— this invention was the first to use this position. Another of the more important patents was one for a combined smoothing and fluting iron, granted on Mar 11, 1873.

NATIONAL IRON DISTRIBUTING COMPANY, 817 Foss Avenue, Drexel Hills, Pa. Marketed the Ne Plus Ultra coke-burning iron, patented by George Finn of Newark in 1902. They later marketed the Onlyone, an improved version of the Ne Plus Ultra. (Fig 121, 122, 166, 167).

NATIONAL STAMPING & ELECTRIC WORKS, Chicago, Ill. Makers of petrol irons under various labels: International, Laundry Maid, and Comfort among them.

NE PLUS ULTRA. See National Iron Distributing Co.

NEW YORK PRESSING IRON COMPANY, New York. Made gas irons from c.1910.

NIELY, Denmark. Maker of tailors' box irons.

NORTH BROTHERS, Philadelphia. Makers of the Crown fluting machine. There was probably a connection between North Bros. and the American Machine Co.

OBER, George H. Chagrin Falls, Ohio. Active c.1870-1920. Several patents granted and irons manufactured. On July 31, 1894 a U.S. Patent was granted for a wooden handle similar in shape to the Mrs. Potts design, and another was issued on May 28, 1895 covering a sleeve iron.

ODELIN, Andre. A french iron manufacturer of the nineteenth century. (Fig 170).

O.K. An English made gas iron. (Fig 171).

O.K. FAMILY LAUNDRY IRON. See Horace P. Carver. (Fig 80).

OLIVE. The name given to a type of latch on charcoal irons made by Grossag.

OMEGA, Thuringia, Germany. A large and important foundry. Made a spirit iron after the Feldmeyer style. (Fig 172).

ONLY-BASE-BURNER. Invented and patented by Thomas F. Hagerty of San Francisco in March 1896 and manufactured by William E. Hoyt, New York, with improvements, in 1898. (Fig 139).

163

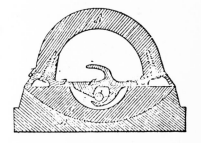

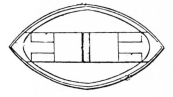

164

163 *Mrs Potts Sad Iron. Patented 1871.*

164 *The drawing from the U.S. patent of April 4, 1871, granted to Mrs Mary Florence Potts, covering a sad iron with a detachable handle.*

167

167

168

170

165

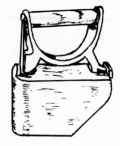
166

171

169   172

165   *Mrs Streeter's Gem Polisher. Double-
       ended and sleeve irons were also available
       for use with the detachable handle.*

166   *Onlyone.*

167   *Onlyone, later model.*

168   *Ober. Late nineteenth century.*

169   *An advertisement for Mrs Potts Patent Iron.*

170   *French sad iron by Andre Odelin.
       Nineteenth century.*

171   *'O.K.', England.*

172   *Spirit iron made by Omega to the design of
       Feldmeyer.*

ONLYONE. Marketed by the National Iron Distributing Co., Drexel Hills, Pa. An improved version of the earlier Ne Plus Ultra. (Fig 166, 167).

ORIGINAL KNOX, The. A crimping machine made by the American Machine Company, Philadelphia, under the patents of Susan R. Knox, granted Apr 26, 1870 and July 3, 1877.

OSBORNE, C. S. Newark, N.J. This was one of the few American manufacturers of goffering irons. The works were established in 1826 but did not use the name of Osborne until 1862. They are still in existence, making small tools.

OTTO. A marque use by William Cross & Co., West Bromwich, for their gas and other irons.

OUR VERY BEST. An American iron of the Potts type carrying the patent dates Oct 13, 1908 and July 5, 1910. There was an identical iron marked Harpers-Chicago and dated Aug 27, 1907. (Fig 140).

PACIFIC HARDWARE & STEEL COMPANY. An American manufacturer or selling company who issued a catalogue in 1902.

PACK, Carl. Erkrath, Germany. Active 1897-1953. Made the Flott charcoal iron in the early 20th century.

PARISIEN, Le. Marque of iron sold by Bazar de l'Hotel de Ville, Paris. A pictorial mark shows a sailing ship with four masts. (Fig 85).

PARTRIDGE, London. A prominent smith who was active in the late seventeenth century and who almost certainly made irons.

PATENT GROUND STAR IRON. Made by the Enterprise Mfg. Co., Philadelphia. The design was patented on Oct 1, 1867 by Arthur Y. Hubbell, who improved it with an inner-insulated handle. It was further improved by a patent granted to J. R. Baker and T. H. Ashbury on Jan 16, 1877 covering a handle insulated and pierced with holes. (Fig 118).

PATENT HOME IRON. An American iron with a rounded heel to polish the front of shirts. (Fig 173).

PEASE, H. S. Potage, Wisc., and Cincinnati, Ohio. Invented a combined fluting and smoothing iron. A U.S. Patent was granted Aug 18, 1885, and another for improvements on Aug 14, 1888. (Fig 174).

PELOUZE MANUFACTURING COMPANY, Chicago, Ill. Made electric irons from c.1912. (Fig 175).

PENN. A fluting machine made by the American Machine Co., Philadelphia.

PERFECT TRAVELLING SPIRIT IRON. Made in England, c.1910. Weights available 2 and 3lb. There were also 'Perfect' laundry irons weighing 4½ and 6½lb. The laundry irons had bell-shaped tanks. (Fig 191).

PETH PRESSING PROCESS. A steam iron with a U.S. Patent granted in 1910. The steam is fed in from an outside source.

PHENSAUL BROTHERS, Plymouth, England. Active at least in the 1850s.

POLAND LAUNDRY MACHINERY COMPANY. Boston, Mass. Makers of commercial laundry machinery. See Tyler Ironer. (Fig 190).

POTTS PATENT IRON. See Mrs. Potts Patent Iron.

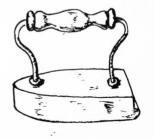

173

174

175

173   *Patent Home Iron. c.1880.*

174   *Pease combined fluting and smoothing iron. The handle is detachable and is used as the fluter with the corrugated plate on the other side of the iron. 1888. (see also Fig 43).*

175   *Pelouze. c.1912.*

176   Rose gas iron.

177   'Royal' petrol iron.

178   Union iron. 1892

PRATT, E. L. Granted U.S. Patent on Dec 13, 1864 covering a grip for an iron which allowed the whole arm of the operator to apply pressure.

PRENTIS, George J. Granted U.S. Patent on Oct 18, 1859, covering a two-handled polishing iron. (Fig 32).

PRESS RITE. An electric neck-tie iron of the 1920s made in the U.S.A. by Cosco Products Corp.

PRICE, A. H. See Arnold, G.B.

PROCTOR-SILEX CORPORATION, U.S.A. Absorbed the Enterprise Mfg. Co. in 1955.

PUFF MASTER. An all-bronze steam iron made by Wilnite-BM-Co., Downey, Calif., between c.1910 and c.1920. It had to be fed with steam from an outside source.

QUEEN CARBON SAD IRON. An American carbon coal-burning iron, similar in shape and style to the Everson double-ended iron.

RADIANT. A petrol iron made by the Akron Lamp & Mfg Co., Akron, Ohio, and marketed by Radiant Products Company, also of Akron.

REIBER. A name given by Grossag to a latch fitted to some of their charcoal-heated irons.

ROBERTS BROTHERS. Prominent Welsh smiths who were active from the 1720s and who almost certainly made irons.

ROBINSON, Thomas, London. An iron foundry that was active from the late seventeenth century until demolished to make way for the building of Victoria station. Almost certainly irons were produced.

ROSA, A. Granted U.S. Patent covering a charcoal iron in 1890.

ROSE IRON. A gas iron patented in 1905 and made by the Rosenbaum Mfg. Co, New York City. (Fig 176).

ROSENBAUM MANUFACTURING COMPANY, New York City. See Rose Iron.

ROSTELL & REKARD, Copenhagen. Early makers of gas irons. (Fig 12).

ROTARY SMOOTHING IRON COMPANY, New York. Makers of a spirit iron for household use—most of this type were intended for travellers. The flame heated the upper surface while the lower surface was being used as the sole. When cool, the entire body was turned over so the top plate became the sole. Made under the patent of Mar 21, 1854, granted to Jeremiah Brown. (Fig 84).

ROYAL SELF-HEATING IRON COMPANY. Big Prairie, Ohio. Makers of the Royal petrol iron. (Fig 177).

ROYER'S FORD IRON FOUNDRY, Royer's Ford, Pa.

SABOLD, John, Boyertown, Pa. Granted U.S. Patent on Oct 4, 1892, covering an iron similar to the Mrs. Potts design. Marketed as the Union iron. (Fig 178).

SALAMANDER. A marque used for a box iron made by Bless & Drake under James F. Bless's U.S. Patent of 1897. (Fig 179).

SALTER & COMPANY, George. West Bromwich. Makers of charcoal irons similar in style to those made by Cannon, Siddons and Kenrick. Salter also manufactured springs, scales and typewriters.

SANGLIER, Le. A marque of French-made sad iron on sale in 1928.

SARTO TECNICA, La. An Italian-made tailor's box iron made at the end of the nineteenth century. (Fig 180).

SAUERBIER & SON, Henry. Newark, N.J. Made a crimping machine under the U.S. Patent of Susan R. Knox, granted on Nov 20, 1866. Sauerbier was granted a U.S. Patent for a crimping machine of his own design on Nov 22, 1870.

SCHWEIGER, J. and E. POST. A charcoal iron with these names also carries the double-headed eagle of Austria. Other marks on the same iron are: 'K-K Metall Waaren Fabrik In Wien 1865'. (Fig 181).

S & C MANUFACTURING COMPANY. Dubuque, Iowa. Made the Mrs. Potts iron after expiration of the patent.

SEELEY, Henry W. Menlo Park, N.J. Granted U.S. Patent covering an electric iron in 1882. This iron was heated by means of carbon sticks. A second patent was granted on Oct 30, 1883 with Richard N. Dyer as collaborator. (Fig 16).

SELLERS & SONS, William. Airedale Works, Keighley, Yorks. The company was founded in 1854.

SENSIBLE. Trade name for irons made by Nelson R. Street, Groton, N.Y. There was a U.S. Patent granted for a Potts type iron carrying this name in 1887. (Fig 192).

SERGEANT, Henry C. Newark, N.J. Granted U.S. Patent covering a crimping machine on Nov 23, 1869, which was made by Lowerre and Tucker, also of Newark, under the trade name Crown Jewel.

SHAW, Huntington. Nottingham and London. A prominent smith active between 1659 and 1710 and who almost certainly made irons.

SHELDON & COMPANY LIMITED, Thomas. Springvale Foundry, near Wolverhampton. Active in 1888, when an iron manufacturers' association was formed (the association lasted until 1894). The company was bought by Archibald Kenrick in 1932. Sheldon listed the Darwin Sad Iron in their 1920 catalogue. (Fig 110).

SHEPARD HARDWARE COMPANY, Buffalo, N.Y. Made fluter with patent dates Nov 12, and Dec 17, 1878. The machine was similar to the Geneva fluter. (Fig 193).

179

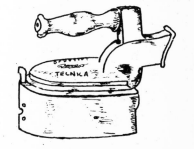

180

181

179   *'Salamander' box iron. U.S.A. 1897.*

180   *La Sarto Tecnica. Early twentieth century.*

181   *Schweiger & Post. 1865.*

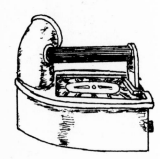

182

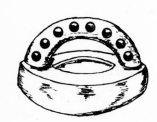

183

182   Charcoal iron by James Smart. 1851.

183   Star Polishing Iron, also known as the
        Chinese Polisher. 1877.

SIDDONS LIMITED, Joseph and Jesse. West Bromwich, Staffs. Active from 1846 to 1939 making irons. The company still exists and makes castings for the motor industry. Catalogued in 1902 was a tailor's charcoal iron of the same design as Bless & Drake in the U.S.A. and also marked with the Hephaestus figure.

Siddons were probably the last foundry to make polishing irons—they listed a convex soled iron until 1939. A trade name was Victoria.

SIEMENS BROTHERS. England. Established in 1842 by Ernst Werner von Siemens and Karl Wilhelm Siemens. Ernst returned to Germany where he established the world famous electrical business. Karl stayed in England and was knighted. A gas iron was produced by Siemens Brothers.

SIMPLEX. An electric iron first patented in 1906. Made by the Simplex Electric Heating Company, Cambridge, Mass. Sold by the American Ironing Machine Company, Chicago, Ill.

SMART MANUFACTURING COMPANY LIMITED, James. England. Issued a catalogue in 1887 but irons were made much earlier. A tailor's box iron was included in the range. (Fig 182).

SMITH, H. & C. King Street Iron Works, Cork. Active at least in the 1850s and 60s.

SMITH AND HAWKES, Eagle Foundry, Broad Street, Birmingham. England. Active 1850s to 1870s.

STANDARD. A spirit iron made by the C. Brown Mfg. Co., Cincinnati, Ohio.

STAR FLUTER. Made by the American Machine Co., Philadelphia, Pa.

STAR POLISHING IRON. Patented Jan 11, 1877 but not catalogued until 1915 by the Enterprise Mfg. Co., Philadelphia. Sometimes called the Chinese Polisher. (Fig 183).

STERLING, C. A. Granted U.S. Patent on Aug 21, 1866 covering a fluting iron made by W. H. Howell under the name Geneva Hand Fluter.

STRAUSE GAS IRON COMPANY, Philadelphia, Pa.

STREETER, Nelson R. Groton, N.Y. Made irons under the marque, Sensible. Granted a patent covering a combined fluting and smoothing iron in 1876 and again in 1878. A Sensible iron similar in design to the Mrs Potts iron was patented by Streeter in 1887. Mrs Streeter's Gem Polisher, and irons for sleeves and flouncing were also produced. (Fig 165).

STUART. Maker of hatters' irons.

SULTANA TOILET IRON. The U.S. Patent covering this iron was granted to Herbert Clayton, New York, on July 4, 1893 and renewed Dec 4, 1900. The fuel was either coal (natural) gas or alcohol and it could double as a lamp. (Fig 93).

SUMMERSCALES & SONS LTD., W. Phoenix Foundry, Keighley, Yorks. Established 1850. Makers of cooking apparatus and laundry machinery. (Fig 184).

SUN MANUFACTURING COMPANY, South Bend, Ind., and Chicago, Ill. Makers of an alcohol iron, the subject of a U.S. Patent granted on Oct 19, 1909. The same castings were used as on the Modern Alcohol Iron, marketed by the Modern Speciality Company, Milwaukee, Wisc. (Fig 185).

SUNSHINE. A petrol iron made c.1917 by the Coleman Co, of Wichita, Kansas. (Fig 94).

SUTTIE & COMPANY, Greenock. Active at least in the 1850s.

SWEENEY IRON. Patented on Nov 17, 1898 and made by Baird & Co., Pittsburgh, Pa. This was not the first patent issued to Mary Sweeney, she was granted a patent covering a polishing iron in November 1896. (Fig 62).

TAGGART, John. Granted U.S. Patent on Sep 9, 1856, covering a charcoal iron with bellows under the handle. (Fig 31).

TALIFERRO & CUMMINGS (inventors). The partnership between Nicholas Taliferro, Augusta, Ky., and William Cummings, Murphyville, Ky. Together they were granted a U.S. Patent on Mar 30, 1852, covering a charcoal iron which was manufactured by Bless & Drake of Newark, N.J. The patent expired c.1866. (Fig 72, 73).

TEINTURIERS, l'Amie des. Paris. A concern which has produced irons for over 100 years, from mid-nineteenth century.

THORNE, Amanda H. Granted U.S. Patent on Feb 9, 1869, covering a standing iron. It is thought to have been the first American patent issued for this type of iron.

TILLY LAMP COMPANY. English manufacturers of petrol burning lamps and other equipment widely used in camping.

TIJOU, Jean. Active in London 1690-1710. Tijou was probably a French refugee in the Netherlands who came to London at the time of William. As a smith from the Low Countries he almost certainly brought iron making methods with him.

TISA. A Mexican made charcoal iron in current production.

TOZOT. A marque used by William Cross & Co., West Bromwich. The Mrs Potts pattern iron was made as the Tozot Heater Box Iron. (Fig 108).

TROY POLISHING IRON. Catalogued by the Chalfant Mfg. Co. in 1881.

TUCKER, Theodore M. A partner in the company of Lowerre & Tucker, Newark, N.J., and patentee of a fluting machine in July 1851.

TULLIS, Boyd W. U.S. Patentee of a cleaning needle and generator of 1929 and 1934. Designer of the Coleman 1940 Model 609.

184

185

186

184   *William Summerscale's rotary laundry ironer. c.1900.*

185   *'Sun' alcohol iron.*

186   *The Turner combined kettle and smoothing iron.*

187

188

189

187 *'Venus'. An Austrian made charcoal iron. Early twentieth century.*

188 *Verebest, U.S.A.*

189 *Walker & Orlynch sleeve iron.*

TURNER, C. C. Granted U.S. Patent on May 8, 1900 covering an iron which could also be used as a kettle. (Fig 186).

TURNER, W. Dublin. Active at least in the 1850s.

TVERDAHL, O. Stoughton, Wisc. With L. D. Clark was granted a U.S. Patent covering the Asbestos iron on May 22, 1900, which was made by the Dover Mfg. Co., Dover, Ohio. (Fig 67, 68).

TYLER IRONER. An ironing machine made by the Poland Laundry Co., Boston, Mass., under a U.S. Patent granted on Mar 4, 1873. The iron itself has a hole in the nose for attachment to the machine. (Fig 190).

UNION. A fluting machine made by the American Machine Company, Philadelphia, Pa.

UNION. Marque of Potts type iron patented by John Sabold on Oct 4, 1892. (Fig 178).

UNIVERSAL THERMO-CELL. A design similar to the Potts iron, patented on June 13, 1911, and made by Landers, Frary & Clark, New Britain, Conn. (Fig 159).

UPHAM, David A. See Worcester Gas Iron Co.

URNER, A. S. See G. B. Arnold.

VAUDIN, John, Le Feurvre Foundry, Bath Street, Jersey. Active at least in the 1850s.

VENUS. An Austrian made charcoal iron, manufactured in the early twentieth century. The iron had an opening sole plate and a 'half floor' cast with the body. It was thereby possible to remove the ashes and leave the fuel in the iron. (Fig 187).

VEREBEST. A gas iron made by George J. Campbell, Philadelphia. (Fig 188).

VICTOR, The. See Horace P. Carver.

VICTORIA. A marque used for a charcoal iron used by J. & J. Siddons Limited.

WALKER, Bernard P., Eagle Foundry, Broad Street, Birmingham, England. Active at least in the 1870s.

WALKER & ORLYNCH (or O. R. LYNCH), Boston, Mass. Makers of a triangular-soled sleeve iron. (Fig 189).

WARD'S QUICK LIGHTING. A petrol iron made by the Akron Lamp and Mfg Co., Akron, Ohio, and marketed by Montgomery Ward, by mail order.

WARWICK, William. See Knauer, D. F.

WESTPHAL, Charles H., Buffalo, N.Y. Patentee of the Buffalo gas iron in 1877. The iron was produced by the Buffalo Forge Company, Buffalo, N.Y. (Fig 78).

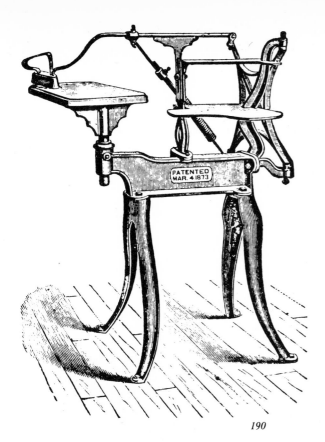

190

191

192

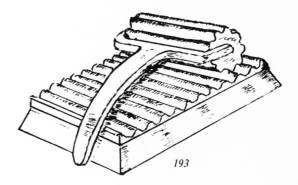

193

190 A

190   *The Tyler Ironer made by The Poland Laundry Machinery Company, Boston, Mass.*

191   *'Perfect' spirit travelling iron. c.1910. This iron was made in England to Feldmeyer's design.*

192   *'Magic' box iron. 1876. A 'Sensible' iron of the same date is of similar shape. The 'Magic' has a removable* slug *and the 'Sensible is solid with a detachable handle.*

193   *Shepard Hardware fluter. 1878.*

WILKINSON, Isaac. Bersham, Denbighshire. Granted patent for a box iron in 1738—probably the first British patent for an iron. The type was still being made in the 1940s. (Fig 6).

WILLIAMS, Adam C. Ravenna, Ohio. Makers of irons marked A.C.W.

WILNITE-BM-COMPANY, Downey, Calif. Made an all-bronze steam iron called the Puff Master. It had to be fed with steam from an outside source. Current between c.1910 and c.1920.

WORCESTER GAS IRON COMPANY, Portland, Maine. Made a gas iron under patent granted to David A. Upham and James J. Fay of Worcester, Mass., from c.1889.

WORCESTER (Mass.) SELF-HEATING FLAT IRON COMPANY. Made the spirit-burning Ideal Self-Heating Flat Iron from c.1890.

WRIGHT. A gas iron listed in the 1912 Butler Brothers catalogue in the U.S.A.

WORKWELL. Marque used by William Cross & Company, West Bromwich.

Chapter Six

IDENTIFICATION POINTS AND MARKS

Apart from founders' trade and series marks, this chapter is concerned with national and individual makers' characteristics.

A C W   The letter marks on irons made by Adam C. Williams of Ravenna, Ohio. (Fig 200).

American Characteristics. Most early American made charcoal irons were equipped with tall smoke stacks, a feature that gradually diminished until the close of the nineteenth century when, with some exceptions, the stack disappeared altogether, replaced by small orifices around the lid.

Anchor emblem. The trade mark of Camion Freres, France. The foundry started making irons in 1820 and is still in existence. (Fig 201).

Anvil emblem. The trade mark of a German made series of charcoal irons in the late nineteenth century. (Fig 202).

Austrian characteristics. Circular handles are indicative of Austrian manufacture. Grossag also made this style in Germany, but usually with some other distinguishing mark such as the Grossag 'G'. (Fig 195, 196).

Belgian characteristics. Nineteenth century Belgian made sad irons had their own particular type of handle resembling a *porter's rest* (a roadside bench supported by two legs). Roses were particularly favoured for decoration. Some French made irons also had these features. Belgian made irons usually had the Dutch type rounded heel. (Fig 203).

Box outline. One of the trademarks of the Colebrookdale foundry in Pennsylvania. (Fig 204).

British characteristics. Early British box irons were usually made from cast steel or cast iron rather than brass as favoured by other European foundries. However, brass-bodied box irons are not unknown from British foundries. (Fig 205, 206).

Bronzing. In the 1870s there grew a widespread belief that brass irons caused yellowing of white cloth. Consequently brass iron sales declined. To overcome this prejudice some iron manufacturers gave their brass irons a coating of bronze. It is reasonably safe to assume that such irons were made post-1870.

194

195

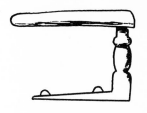

196

194   *American heat-resisting handle. c.1910.*

195   *An example of an Austrian circular handle.*

196   *Austrian handle. Nineteenth century.*

197

198

199

197-199 Three examples of the trade marks used by William Cross & Sons Limited.

Cannon. Trade mark of the Cannon Company of Bilston, Staffordshire but the mark is not found on all their products.

C.C. A mark on some French made charcoal irons, similar in style to other marks: U.C. and U.C.M. Some C.C. irons were sold in Spain but it is thought they were French exports. (Fig 207).

Crane (bird) emblem. Trade mark of C. H. Crane & Company of Wolverhampton. (Fig 208).

Crosses. The Maltese cross with the linked words 'HOT CROSS' was the emblem of William Cross & Sons Limited of West Bromwich. The company also adapted the Maltese cross design for use on the 'Workwell' series of irons and rests. Keeping to the crossed word motif, William Cross used the word 'TOZOT' running vertically and horizontally, and enclosed in a circle, for their mark on that series of irons. (Fig 197-199).

Cross on shield. Trade mark of a Swiss maker of irons active in the latter part of the nineteenth century. (Fig 209).

Devil's head. A decoration used on the handle posts of some German and Austrian irons. (Fig 210).

Diamond outline. One of the trademarks of the Colebrookdale foundry, Pennsylvania. c.1892. (Fig 211).

Dolphins. Some European iron makers favoured dolphin shapes for their handle posts. They should not be taken as a sure means of identification as Grossag, Kaltschmidt, and Max Elb in Germany all used the dolphin, as did Swiss and Spanish makers. The motif probably did not occur until after 1890. (Fig 212-214).

Dutch characteristic. Iron makers in the Netherlands pioneered and continue to make their irons with a round heel. (Fig 215, 216).

EMS 1839. Markings found on some Danish made box irons. (Fig 217).

Eye Irons. The 'eyes' are semi-circular openings in the sides of the body-castings of charcoal irons. They indicate a manufacturing date of after c.1870. Eyes are not a national characteristic. (Fig 249, 250).

'F' under a small crown. The trade mark of the Fredericks-Vaerk foundry, Denmark. (Fig 218).

Fish. A fish passing through a ring was used by Carl Pack of Germany on Flott charcoal irons. (Fig 219).

F.K. (sometimes appearing as E.K.). Initials used by D. F. Knauer on irons patented by him and William Warwick in July 1866. (Fig 221).

Flower. An eight-petalled flower outline design was the emblem of a nineteenth century French maker of double-ended irons. (Fig 220).

French characteristics. A floral design, particularly roses, is indicative of either French or Belgian manufacture. *(continued on p.61)*

MARKS AND CHARACTERISTICS

200

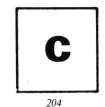

204

208

201

205

209

202

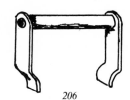

206

210

203

C C

207

211

200 Trade mark of Alan C. Williams.

201 Trade mark of Carnion Freres.

202 Anvil trade mark used by a German foundry.

203 Typical nineteenth century Belgian made sad iron.

204 The box outline trade mark of the Colebrookdale Iron Works.

205 English turned wood box iron handle. Nineteenth century.

206 English hollow handle for sad iron.

207 'C.C.' trade mark of an unidentified European foundry.

208 Trade mark of C. H. Crane & Company.

209 A late nineteenth century Swiss trade mark.

210 A 'devil's head' handle post.

211 The diamond outline trade mark of the Colebrookdale Iron Works.

EMS 1839

217

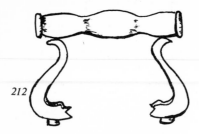

212

F

218

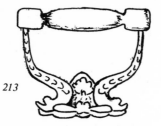

213

219

214

Examples of 'dolphin' handle posts:

220

212   *Eighteenth century Danish*

213   *Max.Elb. c.1898.*

214   *Kaltschmidt. c.1925.*

215   *Typical Dutch made charcoal iron with rounded heel. c.1800.*

216   *'Dutch' style handle as named by German makers.*

217   *'EMS 1839'. A mark observed on a Danish made iron.*

218   *Trade mark of Frederiks-vaerk.*

219   *Trade mark used by Carl Pack on the Flott iron.*

220   *Floral trade mark of a nineteenth century French manufacturer.*

221   *Trade mark of D. F. Knauer.*

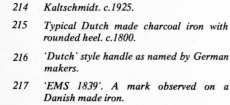

215

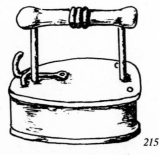

216

F.K. 221

Some early nineteenth century French sad irons were cut from steel plate rather than cast. The upper surface of these cut irons was usually plain, although some did carry modest decoration. A feature of many French made sad irons is the raised lip around the edge. Oil or spirit was poured in and ignited for heating the iron. Some French irons were, and still are, made with hooked handles for hanging on a horizontal bar. As in Belgium, some French sad irons had the 'porters' rest' type of handle. (Fig 222-225).

'G' The symbol of the Grossag foundry in Germany. Apart from the 'G' and sometimes a lion's head, Grossag used, in the late 1920s and '30s, the letters 'F.G.'. One of the forms showed some influence from the Nazi *swastika*. (Fig 226-228).

Hephaestus. The legendary Greek iron worker. His image was used on irons made by Bless & Drake, Newark, N.J., and by J. & J. Siddons, West Bromwich.

HERBULOT and C.H. An entwined C.H. within a wreath and the word HERBULOT enclosed in a box are identification marks of a nineteenth century French manufacturer. (Fig 229).

Hinges at the side. After c.1850 some charcoal irons had lids which were hinged at the side. However, hinges at the rear continued to be popular.

Hollow handles. Hollow handles which would retain the heat less than solid were introduced on British made sad irons in the late nineteenth century. (Fig 206).

'HP 25'. Marks found on some German made charcoal irons. The significance is not known. (Fig 230).

Italian characteristics. For charcoal irons Italian makers particularly favoured pictorially decorated lids for charcoal irons. They also used Swiss style fire box castings with holes around the base. (Fig 231).

J.B.M. The initials of J. B. Mast, New York, suppliers of hatters' irons in the nineteenth century. (Fig 232).

J.M. Those initials within a circle were the identification marks of a French sad iron maker still in production in the 1930s. The trade name used was Le Sanglier. (Fig 233).

K The single letter K in a circle was used as an emblem by Karl Kaltschmidt of Germany. (Fig 234).

Keystone. A polishing iron of c.1880 made by the Colebrookdale Iron Company of Pottstown, Pa., used an outline of a keystone as an emblem. The iron was also made in Great Britain. (Fig 235).

Lion, rampant. A mark on an Italian made charcoal iron of the early twentieth century. It also carries the words 'Brevetto - Italy'. (Fig 236).

222

223

224

225

222   *French 'hook-on' handle. Nineteenth century.*

223   *French handle. Twentieth century.*

224   *French handle for sad iron. Nineteenth century.*

225   *Typical French sad iron of the Nineteenth century.*

G 226

HP 25 230

 233

 227

 234

 231

 228

226/7   *Trade marks used by Grossag.*

228   *Style of charcoal iron handle similar to the Swiss but made by Grossag in Germany— the 'dolphin' posts face inwards.*

229   *Herbulot trade mark.*

230   *'HP 25' mark observed on a sad iron.*

231   *Typical Italian made charcoal iron. c.1905.*

232   *Trade mark of J. B. Mast.*

233   *'JM' trade mark of a French manu-facturer.*

234   *Trade mark of Karl Kaltschmidt.*

235   *Keystone outline trade mark of the Colebrookdale Iron Works.*

236   *Rampant lion trade mark of an Italian maker.*

 235

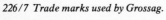 HERBULOT 229

JBM 232

 236

Lion, standing. This was used as a trade mark by a nineteenth century French maker of irons. (Fig 242).

Lion's head. An emblem used by the German foundry of Grossag. (Fig 243).

LYNG. A series name of William Cross & Sons Limited of Wolverhampton. (Fig 244).

MAGNET. Either or both as an emblem and lettering. The trade mark of the General Electric Company. (Fig 245).

Mascot latch knobs. On German and Austrian made charcoal irons it became a tradition in the twentieth century for the knob operating the latch to be cast in some decorative form, usually a human head or a bird. Study of these and their significance would be an interesting line of research. (Fig 246).

Monster's head. Charcoal irons with the chimney in the shape of a monster's head were made by Berliner Industries and other German makers in the 1920s and '30s.

ODELIN and A.O. An entwined A.O. within a wreath and surmounted by a crown was the mark of a nineteenth century manufacturer in France. (Fig 247).

Patterned soles. A U.S. patent was granted on Nov 28, 1876 to Michael Mahony, covering a sad iron with a diamond pattern embossed on the sole. The purpose of this was to polish starched material to achieve a high sheen. Mahony used several designs other than the diamond pattern.

Portuguese characteristics. A straight smoke stack on charcoal burning irons is not observed on the products of other countries. Portugese foundries did, however, sometimes make irons with side and forward pointing smoke stacks. (Fig 251).

Post Horn. The outline of a post horn is the emblem of a nineteenth century French maker of sad irons. (Fig 248).

Registered designs. Registered design marks are useful where British made irons of between 1842 and 1883 are concerned. Not many irons are so marked but when it is carried it is a useful key to dating. The mark was a diamond with the letters 'Rd.' in the centre. Between 1842 and 1867 a key letter for the year was carried within the top corner of the diamond. From 1868 until 1883 the key letter was carried within the right-hand corner. The key letters are coded as follows:
1842 X, 1843 H, 1844 C, 1845 A, 1846 I, 1847 F, 1848 U, 1849 S, 1850 V, 1851 P, 1852 D, 1853 Y, 1854 J, 1855 E, 1856 L, 1857 K, 1858 B, 1859 M, 1860 Z, 1861 R, 1862 O, 1863 G, 1864 N, 1865 W, 1866 Q, 1867 T, 1868 X, 1869 H, 1870 C, 1871 A, 1872 I, 1873 F, 1874 U, 1875 S, 1876 V, 1877 P, 1878 D, 1879 Y, 1880 J, 1881 E, 1882 L, 1883 K.
　　The letters and figures in the other corners of the diamond indicate the

237

238

237-238 Examples of British Registered Design marks.

239

240

SF

241

day and month of registration and the 'bundle'. The letter in the circle at the head of the diamond shows the class of goods. (Fig 237, 238).

Romulus and Remus pictorial motif. The twins being suckled by a she-wolf is carried as an emblem on some Italian made charcoal irons. (Fig 239).

Scandinavian characteristics. Sad irons from Scandinavian foundries normally have tall handle posts which are not cast into the body of the iron but are riveted through the single-piece strap. (Fig 240).

S.F. Initials used by a French or Belgian manufacturer in the mid-nineteenth century. (Fig 241).

S.F.N.G.R. The letters carried on a banner over a globe formed the emblem of a French or Belgian manufacturer of irons in the nineteenth century. (Fig 252).

Shield outline. A trademark of the Colebrookdale foundry in Pennsylvania. (Fig 257).

Spanish characteristics. Shallow body castings for charcoal irons. (Fig 250).

Stars. A five-pointed star has been used as an emblem by several manufacturers:
W. H. Howell, Chicago, Ill.
Colebrookdale Iron Works, Pennsylvania.
Enterprise Mfg Co., Philadelphia, for the Patent Ground Star Iron.
By some Italian manufacturers.
A six-pointed star was sometimes used by Grossag of Germany. (Fig 254).

Swallow or Martin (bird). This bird shown in flight was the emblem of a French or Belgian maker of irons in the nineteenth century. (Fig 256).

Swiss characteristics. The Swiss manufacturers favoured making charcoal irons with the body casting square-sided and carried to a diamond point at the front. However, Grossag in Germany made irons in this style, calling the series 'Germania'.(Fig 249).

Tailor's goose. A way of judging the age of a tailor's goose is by the handle. Generally, the longer the handle the older the goose.

U.C. A mark on a charcoal iron. The example also carries a pictorial representation of a Spanish castle on the heat shield. Possibly made in France for export. Similar in style to letter 'C.C.' and 'U.C.M.' found on other irons. (Fig 258).

U.C.M. A mark on a charcoal iron. Possibly made in France for export. See also 'C.C.' and 'U.C.' (Fig 259).

The study of manufacturers' marks and characteristics is a field of research that offers a very wide interest to collectors and the foregoing is but a brief sample of what can be found. It is only by enthusiastic exchange of information that anything like a comprehensive guide to identification can ever be compiled.

239   *Romulus & Remus trade mark on an Italian made charcoal iron.*

240   *Norwegian sad iron with typical Scandinavian tall handle.*

241   *Trade Mark of French or Belgian foundry.*

242

243

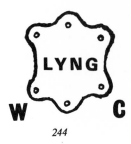

244

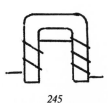

245

246

247

249

250

248

242   Lion trade mark of a French foundry.

243   Lion's head emblem used by Grossag on some charcoal iron handle posts.

244   The 'Lyng' trade mark of Wm. Cross & Sons Ltd.

245   'Magnet' trade mark of the General Electric Company.

246   German charcoal iron by Grossag— 1890-c.1935.

247   Trade mark of Andre Odelin.

248   A post iron trade mark used by a French foundry.

249   Typical Swiss charcoal iron. Late nineteenth century.

250   Typical Spanish charcoal iron. Twentieth century.

MARKS AND CHARACTERISTICS

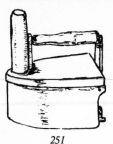

251

256

260

252

257

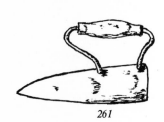

258

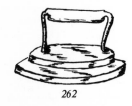

261

251 Portuguese charcoal iron with straight smoke stack. Early twentieth century.

252 Trade mark of French or Belgian foundry.

253 Trade mark of George Salter & Company.

254/5 Star-shaped trade marks:
Five-pointed stars were used on the Patent Ground Star Iron, and on Irons made by W. H. Howell, and by the Colebrookdale Iron Works.

The six-pointed star was used by Grossag.

256 Swallow trade mark used by a French foundry.

257 Shield outline trade mark of the Colebrookdale Iron Works.

258/9 'UC' and 'UCM' marks observed on European made irons.

260 Oriental charcoal iron—modern.

261 A typical sleeve iron of the nineteenth century.

262 European lace iron of the nineteenth century. The indistinct markings show 'I.W.(?).I'.

263 A European box lace iron, 4.5 cm long.

253

259

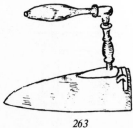

262

254

255

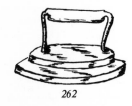

263

264

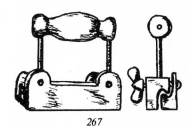

267

268

265

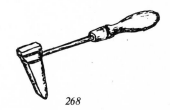

269

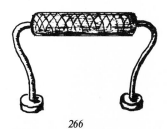

266

270

264   *German style handle. Nineteenth century.*

265   *American handle of c.1870—George H. Ober.*

266   *American handle—Colebrookdale foundry. foundry.*

267   *Hatter's 'shackle' for forming brims.*

268   *Dutch hatter's slug heated box iron.*

269   *Hatter's iron. Early nineteenth century.*

270   *Hatter's iron. Mid-nineteenth century.*

APPENDIX I
CHARACTERISTIC SOLES

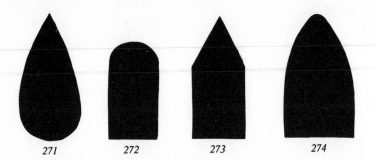

271   272   273   274

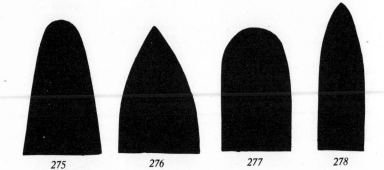

275   276   277   278

CHARACTERISTIC SOLES.

271   *Dutch.*

272   *Danish.*

273   *Swiss.*

274   *English.*

275/6 *French.*

277   *French polishing iron.*

278   *Sleeve iron.*

279   *Mrs Potts Patent Iron.*

280   *Electric iron—G.E.C. Magnet. c.1935.*

281   *Billiard table iron.*

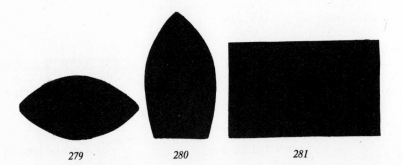

279   280   281

APPENDIX II
CLASSIFICATION OF SMOOTHING IRONS AND APPROXIMATE DATES OF INTRODUCTION

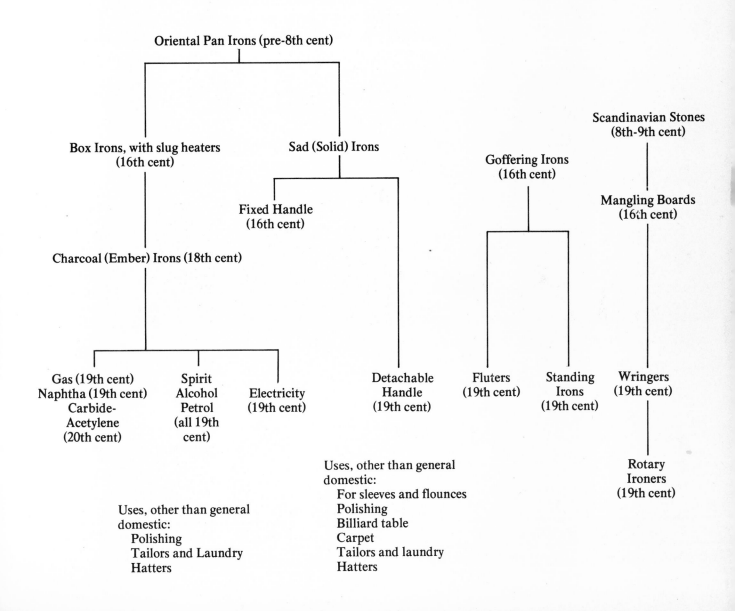

APPENDIX III

MUSEUMS AND COLLECTIONS

ARNHEM, Holland: Het Nederlands Openluchtmuseum.

BIRMINGHAM, England: The Birmingham City Museums.

BURFORD, Oxon., England: Cotswold Folk and Agricultural Museum (open by appointment).

COPENHAGEN, Denmark: Dansk Museum.

HALIFAX, Shibden Hall, England: West Yorkshire Folk Museum.

HAUGESUND, Norway: Haugesund Museum.

LONDON: The Science Museum.

OKEHAMPTON, Sticklepath, Devon, England: The Finch Foundry Trust.

OSLO, Norway: Norsk Folkemuseum.

ROUEN, France: Musee le Secq des Tournelles.

WASHINGTON DC, U.S.A.: Museum of History and Technology, The Smithsonian Institution.

YORK, England: The Castle Museum.

ACKNOWLEDGEMENTS

The publishers wish to express their gratitude to Carol Edwards of Granny Goods, East Molesey and Mrs E. M. Spark of Cobham, Surrey for the loan of irons for illustrative purposes and for their advice and encouragement.

Appreciation is also extended to Archibald Kenrick & Son Limited, West Bromwich for illustrations and advice.

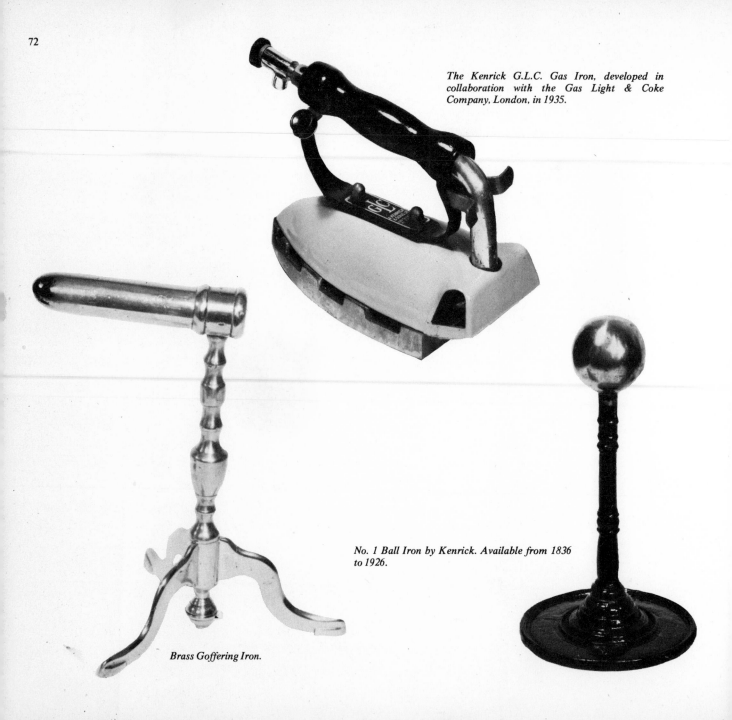

The Kenrick G.L.C. Gas Iron, developed in collaboration with the Gas Light & Coke Company, London, in 1935.

No. 1 Ball Iron by Kenrick. Available from 1836 to 1926.

Brass Goffering Iron.